Ms. Judy Weverka
1106 Waller Rd.
Brentwood, TN 37027

Mystery of Color

by Rosemary Sadez Friedmann

L&M Publications, Naples, Florida

Published by:
L&M Publications
PMB 229
PO Box 413005
Naples, Florida 34103-3005

Mystery of Color
By Rosemary Sadez Friedmann

Copyright ©2003 by Rosemary Sadez Friedmann

All rights reserved. No part of this book may be reproduced or transmitted in any form or by any means electronic or mechanical, including photocopying, recording or by any information storage and retrieval system without written permission from the publisher.

Library of Congress Cataloging-in-Publication Data

Sadez Friedmann, Rosemary.
    Mysery of color: inspiration for developing your own interior style/Rosemary Sadez Friedmann.
    p. cm.
    ISBN 0-9714897-6-9

    1. Color in interior decoration. 2. Interior decoration —Amateurs' manuals. 1. Title.

NK2115.5.C6S24 2003   747'.94
                               QB133-614

Edited by Gail M. Kearns, GMK Editorial & Writing Services, Santa Barbara, California
Book design by Peri Poloni, Knockout Design, Cameron Park, California
Art Direction by Penelope C. Paine, Santa Barbara, California
Fabric designs by Dennis Spangler, Santa Barbara, California

Printed in China

To the Spirit of Love

Dive Deep, O mind, dive deep in the ocean of God's beauty! If you descend to the uttermost depths, there you will find the gem of love. —Bengali Hymn

Contents

Acknowledgments 6

Introduction 7

Chapter One—Color History 8

Chapter Two—Color Palettes 16

Chapter Three—Color Wheel 28

Chapter Four—Color Psychology . .38

Chapter Five—Color Healing 56

Chapter Six—Color Properties . . .70

Chapter Seven—Color Light 82

Chapter Eight—Color Discovery . .94

Chapter Nine—Color Language . .104

Chapter Ten—Color Cycles 116

Chapter Eleven—Color Questions 126

Chapter Twelve—Color Success . .134

Resources & Recommended
Reading 142

Acknowledgments

Thank you, Abo and Aba, my parents, for always believing in me and showing me how to love and live with great intensity.

Bob, my devoted husband, without whom life would be truly colorless.

Lisa and Mike, my children, who light up my world and are the greatest rainbows in my life.

Mackenzie, my granddaughter, who colors my world with indescribable happiness.

Olga and Emilio, my sister and brother, who've colored my life all my life.

Fr. Parrott, without whose intercession I would be lost.

Terry O', who knows this book is his fault.

And finally, thank you to all whose prayers made this book possible.

Introduction

The intent of this book is to bring the reader to an understanding of color from an interior design perspective. This book is not meant to educate on all there is about color, but rather to give a general overview of the various aspects of color and how those aspects might fit into our lives.

Am I an expert on color? Yes and no. My field is interior design and so my studies of and experience with color make me at least more knowledgeable than those whose careers fall elsewhere. The color modeling systems used by those in other disciplines, such as graphic design, are valid and will be mentioned here in sidebars so as to bring awareness to you, the reader, but for our intent and purpose we are mainly concerned with expressing ourselves with color in the home.

Some even say that an interior designer is akin to an art director, set designer, installation artist. From that experience and expertise, this book has been written.

Are you an expert on color? Absolutely. You really *do* know what you like even if you don't think you do. By reading this book you will travel through time, experience cultures, learn things about color you might not have known before and be better able to understand your likes, dislikes and emotional response to certain colors. Enjoy the journey.

Rosemary Sadez Friedmann

Chapter One

Color
History

A History Lesson

Ready for a short history lesson? Okay, here goes. Centuries ago, color, as we know it, was a luxury and reflected early man's view of beauty, grandeur and religion. There were no Porter Paint stores or Sherwin Williams' shops on every other corner. The colors on buildings were simply the color of the materials used such as stone, brick, clay, wood or whatever was available locally. For example, it's been said that the top of the Great Pyramid was a bright colored stone, perhaps actual gold. However, lack of applied color didn't seem to be of consequence. The pyramids of Egypt were made of limestone yet the sharp geometry of the figures produced light and dark shades when caressed by the sun. The absence of added color had its advantages in that the buildings blended well with the environment, and were generally cheap to maintain and resilient to weather. Even when paint was applied to buildings, the colors were made up of natural earth elements, that is, from various iron ores and oxides, so the color selections also blended well with the environment.

In ancient Egypt, colors were deeply connected with religion. Yellow and gold were deified and sacred. In ancient Greece and Rome, brides and priests wore yellow because it was considered a color of the divine. In Japan, gold was thought to be the color of heaven.

The Romans decorated their temples with colored marble from their quarries, which were red, green, black and white. Meanwhile, the Muslims were adorning their mosques with mosaic tiles of turquoise, gold and blue.

It is believed that color, when used, was mostly for decoration and religious symbolism. For example, the Tower of Babel was thought to have been painted in a different strong hue for each symbolic step toward Heaven. Is that true? We have no eyewitnesses available today but it does paint an interesting picture in our heads. In decoration, each color had a purpose or meaning. In temples of Egypt, green like the valley of the Nile was used for floors and also for columns to represent growth of plants. Intensely blue images of Heaven carrying bright yellow stars twinkle from the ceilings of those shrines.

Only in ancient Crete is it known that art was created for art's sake, without any religious meaning. Paintings on walls were done to give the effect of picture windows. They used cheerful colors in both their impressionistic and figurative motifs (lots of flying fish) as well as the more ornamental patterns on ceilings, walls and columns.

Design Tip

Use of cool color combinations will make a room look calm, clean and crisp. Example: Soft blue walls with upholstery in green, blue and violet.

Blue emerged as a decorative hue way back in 4500 B.C. in Mesopotamia. The lapis lazuli, an azure-blue semi-precious stone, supposedly had restorative and life-giving powers. King Tut's jewelry was made of gold and lapis lazuli. Egyptian mummies were often wrapped in blue cloth. Those guys really knew how to dress up, didn't they?

Bright blue threads were used in age-old Peruvian embroideries. Blue linen was unearthed in the caves where the Dead Sea scrolls were discovered. Tibetans often used indigo, a deep violet-blue, in their prayer scrolls.

Blue symbolized immortality to the ancient Chinese. For the Romans it was black. The Japanese see black as the color of solemnity and mystery, expressing the depth of the unknown.

Five thousand years ago you couldn't go to your local home store to buy paint, but you could make your own. Well, more or less. In Egypt, grinding, mixing and oiling the various elements made colors. Green was made from malachite. Blue came from turquoise. Black and white were easy; they just used soot for black and chalk or limestone for white. Browns and yellows came from soil. And we were taught not to play in the mud! Was our creativity stifled at a young age?

Color was very symbolic back when togas were in vogue. In Egypt, purple was the color of earth as interpreted from hieroglyphics. White was a symbol of dominance; hence the Pharaohs wore white crowns when expressing dominance. A red crown was worn to proclaim rulership.

In Judaism, God was represented by the use of a rainbow. Color, in that case, was used instead of giving a name or using an image for the Supreme Being, which were both forbidden in that religion.

Early Greeks recognized four elements: fire, earth, water and air. Aristotle gave these elements color. Fire was yellow, water and air, when pure, were white. He also gave white to earth explaining that the variations of color in earth come from tincture. He further explains this theory by reminding us that ashes, which are the final element of earth, are white. No, they are gray, you say? Aristotle was posed that question also, and responded with the fact that more tinting, an active principle in the process of combustion, causes the gray in the smoke. Who's to argue with Aristotle?

12

The Chinese more or less agreed with the Greeks but added their own twist. They eliminated air as an element of color and added wood and metal. So from the Chinese viewpoint, elements were earth, depicted as yellow, fire as red, water as black, wood as green and metal as white.

Oops, there's another opinion. Ancient Jewish historians associated white with earth, red with fire, and water was purple and air (back in vogue) was yellow.

Color in ancient marriage rites was very symbolic. The Jewish marriage ceremony was performed under the talis, which was a golden silk prayer shawl supported by pillars. The bride would walk around these pillars seven times in memory of the siege of Jericho. The Hindu bride had her own ritual. Six days before the big event, she would wear old, tattered yellow clothes to drive away all evil spirits. She wore yellow again on her wedding day, and once married, she would always wear yellow every time her husband returned from a long trip.

In China, the bride wore red and her garment was embroidered with dragons. More red for the Chinese bride awaited her. She was carried in a red chair to the ceremony and that chair was adorned with the groom's family name in, guess what color? Red. Still more red. The bride and groom toasted during the ceremony with wine in two goblets that were tied together with red ribbon. The bride held a red umbrella and firecrackers were exploded after the ceremony.

Design Tip

Never give two or more colors equal importance in a room. Let one dominate while the other plays sidekick. And never use a color just once.

Red was considered a love potion in the Dutch East Indies. The name of a boy or girl was written on white paper with red blood from a red hen. If someone would touch that name, they'd become infatuated with the person whose name they touched. Worth a try, perhaps.

Legend has it that red was the first color perceived by man. The Egyptians used red ochre to color their bodies, walls and fabrics. During medieval times, only nobility was allowed to wear red coats. It was a sign of power.

In ancient times, orange had many implied meanings. It was a color that represented love, both earthly and heavenly, but it also symbolized avenged infidelity. Helen of Troy had to wear orange garments because of her affair with Paris. Even during the Middle Ages bright orange was the symbol for false love, deceit and disloyalty.

The regal connotations of purple are well known. Alexander the Great was a great fan of purple. But, in those times, beware the wearer of purple other than the highest state officials. They were suspiciously regarded as plotters looking to overthrow regimes. There are numerous mentions of purple in the Old Testament, where it is associated with pomp and circumstance.

And let's not forget white. In Greek fables, the all-powerful gods lived on the snow-capped mountains. Although often considered as no color, the Egyptians saw white differently. For them it was a blazing color and they dubbed it "a lady of strength."

Obviously, there are many symbolic and cultural associations to color, which even today may have something to do with how a person reacts to a certain color. But it wasn't until the Renaissance period that color really developed to personify much of our attitude about color and beauty in modern times.

This history is but a brief introduction to the many faces of color. As you will see, there's more to color than meets the eye.

Chapter Two

Color
Palettes

"In visual perception a color is almost never seen as it really is—as it physically is. This fact makes color the most relative medium in art."

—Josef Albers, painter and author of *Interaction of Color*

Color is perhaps the most potent ingredient available to artists, from the mere amateur, dabbling in it for personal entertainment, right up to the preeminent celebrated masters. The palettes of artists throughout history have varied so much that it can be fascinating and enlightening to take a look at color from their perspectives. How about a short art lesson?

The art of oil painting, as we know it today, began in the fifteenth century when oil paints were invented. This made it possible for artists to mix and blend colors on a palette. Cennino Cennini, a mid-fifteenth century Florentine writer, wrote *The Craftsman's Handbook*, the earliest surviving Italian treatise on painting, known in Italian as *Il Libro dell'Arte*. Like a meticulous recipe book, it is extremely thorough in its description of how the Old Masters painted, the materials they used, how they got their pigments and about the techniques they used in their paintings.

The Italian Renaissance artist Leonardo da Vinci taught us a lot about what we know today regarding color. He enlightened us to the fact that if you take a body of white (a sheet, paint, fabric) and divide it in two, both halves being equal in whiteness, and place one on a medium colored background and the other on a dark background, the one on the dark background will appear whiter. The darker background will also appear darker behind the white than on its own. Contrast is inherent in what da Vinci illustrated for us.

It follows then that the perceived value of brightness is commensurate with the perceived value of darkness backing it. Yellow

against red will be brighter than yellow against orange. Let's take this concept home—to be more specific, consider a cottage by the sea. Picture a room that has crisp white walls, white sheer draperies blowing in the breeze of an open window, whitewashed hardwood floors. Now place a love seat upholstered in bright blue and white and throw a few bold yellow and red pillows on it. Toss a bright red area rug in front of the love seat and you have the beginnings of a room that expresses Da Vinci's theory of contrast.

Complementary colors are called such because they bring out the best in each other. On this, Da Vinci had to say, "Of different colors equally perfect, that will appear most excellent which is seen near its direct contrary: a pale color against red; a black upon white . . . blue near yellow; green near red: because each color is more distinctly seen, when opposed to its contrary, than to any other similar to it." That's a mouthful, which, if given poetic license, simply says that opposites attract, or, in the case of interior design, opposites are attractive. Red and green plaid upholstery has great eye appeal. You don't necessarily have to like red and green plaid but when viewing it, the color combination does excite the eye.

If we now follow the above concept of contrast, the next theory becomes obvious. We know that to represent great darkness, contrast it with great light. Again, pale yellow will cause red to appear more intensely red than if you place that same red near purple. To create harmony, arrange three color hues such as yellow, white and blue. There's crispness established where one color leaves off and another one begins, yet the intermingling is harmonious and stimulating. Try deep violet, red-orange and bright green. Invigorating, isn't it? We've taken two contrasting hues and added an intermediary one.

Da Vinci believed that Nature was the truest consultant for color. He was one of the first to use color combinations and mixtures to create his art. Da Vinci's palette contained pure

black, white, red, yellow, green and blue hues. As a painter he was most interested in sunlight, shadows, illumination, spatial relationships and three-dimensional form. Like other artists of his time, he aspired to create roundness, depth and dimension on a flat surface. In his exploration he developed the chiaroscuro style, a method for applying value to a two-dimensional piece of artwork to create the illusion of depth and a three-dimensional solid form. Before Da Vinci came along, artists mixed black and white in their colors to get the effects of light and shadow. But Leonardo would have none of this—he didn't use white or black—his hues were pure in color. The rich colors you see in his work are the result of his technique. Raphael, another great master, also used this system.

El Greco kept his tones somewhat pure as well, but his expression of color was different than Da Vinci's chiaroscuro style. He used large expressive color areas with rich deep tones and chalky tints. El Greco's paintings are highly charged and some say even hypnotic. Have you ever stared at one of his paintings? There is a bit of Mezmorization in them. The haunting intensity of his works is the result of unnaturally long figures and the use of strong color contrasts. Let's bring El Greco's theory into the living room. Make it a two-story living room where the ceiling is about 22 feet above the floor. Paint the walls yellow ochre. That's bold already. Put a fireplace on one wall. Add a metal art relief above it that is custom made to extend by means of leggy spirals from the top of the fireplace to about five feet from the ceiling. The metal is painted in oranges and browns with highlights in cobalt blue. Get the El Greco picture?

Rembrandt's color expression more closely resembled da Vinci's chiaroscuro style, however, blue was absent from his palette, giving his work its luminosity and golden light. He

mainly used white as accents and rarely mixed white with yellow, red, green or brown. He was a master of light and shadow. In his popular painting *"The Night Watch,"* painted in 1642, where he depicts a group of city guardsmen, the canvas is full of color, movement and light. In the foreground are two men, one in bright yellow, and the other in black. The shadow of one man's color tones down the lightness of the other. To the left of the man in black is a little girl dressed in yellow.

Let's jump ahead to Romanticism, a movement in the arts that flourished in the early nineteenth century. It was actually a reaction against Neoclassicism. A battle of wills perhaps that resulted in two great, though contrary philosophies. These two movements covered roughly a century, from about 1750 to 1850. Romanticism emphasized the emotions whereas Neoclassicism advocated more of a restraint of emotion. Some of the best-known artists associated with Romanticism include Eugene Delacroix, John Constable, J.M.W. Turner and William Blake. They filled their canvases with rich color, dynamic brushwork, and often dramatic and emotive subject matter. Take a look at Goya and his depiction of the horrors of war and you will see examples of this. In the U.S., the most important Romantic Movement was the Hudson River School, which was the First American school of Landscape painting. These Romantic artists renounced the passivity

> *"You must observe under which aspect a color appears at its finest in nature; when it receives reflections, or when it is lit, or when it has medium shadows, or when they are dark, or when it is transparent."*
> —Leonardo da Vinci

and cool reasoning of classicism, which was the established art of the times. Believe it or not, later on, Impressionism found its roots in the Romantic tradition. I wonder if they called it "retro" back then.

How are we doing? Are we bored or fascinated? Let's continue our brief art lesson with more theories on color, which appeared in the 1800s. Johann Wolfgang Goethe, widely recognized as one of the greatest German writers, completed his extensive *Zur Farbenlehre* in 1810 (translated as *Goethe's Theory of Colours*), which he sometimes called his single most important work. In it, he gives an exposition of his own theory of color, debates the Newtonian theory that white light is a mixture of colors, and presents a collection of materials on the history of color theory from antiquity to his own time.

In 1810, the same year Goethe's *Theory of Colors* was published, another man named Philipp Otto Runge presented his work on a color-sphere. He dealt mainly with the basic colors of blue, red and yellow alongside black and white. Runge hoped to capture the harmony of colors and wasn't so concerned with the proportions of mixing colors as, say, other color theorists of the time were. Isn't it just like an artist to have to have his or her own particular idiosyncratic way?

In 1839, French chemist Michel Eugene Chevreul published his book *On the Harmony and Contrast of Colors*, which documented observations about color that he made while working as director of dyeing at the Gobelin Tapestry Works, a famous carpet manufacturer. Chevreul established that the look of any color could be totally altered by changing the colors placed immediately next to it. **Color is Relative.** Sounds like something Da Vinci had already noted. Chevreul also observed that colors appear to be at their most intense when positioned directly next to their complements—for example, red makes green look greener when placed next to it.

Sounds again like another Da Vinci discovery. Chevreul called his theory the "law of simultaneous contrast."

French artist Georges Seurat studied the theory of Chevreul before developing Neo-Impressionism (also known as divisionism, pointillism or confetiism), a system of painting in small dots of diversely colored pigments. This is where the brain blends the colors automatically in the involuntary process of optical mixing. Seurat used pure colors applied in thousands of little dots to get the increased brilliance through optical mixing that you see in his paintings. "A Sunday Afternoon on the Island of La Grande Jatte," which hangs in the Art Institute of Chicago, is a good example of this. In this work, he deliberately moved toward a brighter palette. In essence, Seurat purposely applied Chevreul's theory in this and other canvases.

Neo-Impressionism was the movement in painting that was an outgrowth of and reaction to Impressionism. Chevreul's work influenced not only the Neo-Impressionist movement, but also Impressionism and Orphic Cubism. It is interesting to note that with Chevreul's studies, this is the first time that the active role of the brain in the formation of colors was truly introduced in a color system. So finally Chevreul has his very own personal discovery without Da Vinci beating him to the punch.

Many of the Impressionists and Neo-Impressionists eliminated white, black and brown from their palettes. Pissarro, one of the earliest Impressionists, dismissed blacks, browns and ochers, especially dark yellow, entirely. He is known to have told Cézanne to paint only with the three primary colors and their immediate by-product. Other painters of the time, such as Monet and Renoir, mixed and blended colors to produce tone variations, but they used them mostly for accents.

Remember how Da Vinci was very interested in nature, particularly sunlight? Monet followed suit when he painted his *"Cathedral Series."* Monet painted these canvases each hour of the day so he could make changes in the color of the light. Vincent van Gogh, one of the greatest colorists of the Impressionist era, once said, "Keep your love of nature, for that is the true way to learn to understand art more and more."

Speaking of Van Gogh, he had an interesting, ever-changing palette. It seems he was more willing to experiment and he was apt to paint quickly. His early paintings were dark and gloomy, but after his exposure to Impressionism his palette changed significantly and contained intense hues of red, orange, yellow, green and blue. He is quoted as saying, " . . . instead of trying to reproduce exactly what I see before my eyes, I use color more arbitrarily so as to express myself forcibly." No wonder his works are so powerful on the eye and the imagination.

Cézanne, another Neo-Impressionist, got away from the pointillism of his peers and became more inspired with mass and solid form than lighting effects. His palette consisted of colors that were more muted as he moved toward the cold-warm theme.

After the Impressionists came the Fauvist movement led by Henri Matisse. He was captivated by color and used a wide variety of colors in his palette including several shades of yellow, various reds, blues and green. His paintings are always bright and colorful.

The Cubists' work on the other hand was often monochromatic, as they were more energized by shape and newfangled ideas than by color. The basic palette of Cubist George Braque was fairly subdued and contained earthy reds, browns, greens and ochers. According to the *French Encyclopedia* of

1935, his palette averaged sixteen colors. Fellow Cubist Fernand Léger had a much bolder palette and tended to use subtle shading in his work.

Piet Mondrian, who developed the de Stijl movement, sooner or later used pure yellow, red and blue, plus black and white. De Stijl validated pure abstraction and simplicity—form reduced to the rectangle and other geometric shapes, and color to the primary colors, along with black and white, as stated above. Mondrian published a manifesto titled "Neo-Plasticism" in 1920. Another colleague, painter Theo van Doesburg, had initiated a journal titled *De Stijl* in 1917, which spread the

"Art imitates nature and is therefore the grandchild of God."
—Dante

theories of the group. Their work is known to have had tremendous influence on the Bauhaus, and the International Style.

Here's an interesting twist on color. Kandinsky, a teacher and painter at the famous Bauhaus school, proposed that yellow was akin to the shape of a triangle, red to the shape of a square and blue was symbolic of a circle. Johannes Itten, a Swiss painter and teacher of the art of color, joined the staff of the Weimar Bauhaus in 1919, where he formed a friendship with Albers, Klee and Kandinsky. Many of the theories formulated by Itten during his long teaching career were published in 1961 in *The Art of Color,* which for some remains one of the most important textbooks on color.

Then there were the Surrealists like Salvador Dali. They encompassed the twentieth century avant-garde art movement that originated in the revolutionary ideas of Dadaism

25

founded by French writer André Breton, who wrote three manifestos about Surrealism and opened a studio for "surrealist research." According to Breton, Surrealism was a means of uniting conscious and unconscious realms of experience so completely that the world of dream and fantasy would be joined to the everyday rational world in "an absolute reality, a surreality."

Perhaps this quote by Carl Jung, though not a Surrealist himself, best describes the mind of the Surrealist artist:

The creative process, so far as we are able to follow it at all, consists in the unconscious activation of an archetypal image and elaborating and shaping the image into the finished work. By giving it shape, the artist translates it into the language of the present and so makes it possible for us to find our way back to the deepest springs of life.

Surrealism appeals to the subconscious mind by stimulating the imagination through the portraying of a scene in a dream-like manner. Much of Surrealist art is painted with bright, clean colors and great contrasts. Do you think these artists dreamt in color?

Abstract Expressionism, sometimes referred to as Action Painting, was a movement that originated in the 1940s with Arshile Gorky, but became popular in the 1950s when Jackson Pollock appeared on the scene and rendered his infamous *One*, mainly by pouring and splattering paint on the huge canvas. He and others in the movement, including Wassily Kandinsky, Paul Klee, Hans Hoffman, Adolph Gottlieb, Mark Rothko, Willem de Kooning, and a host of others, were trying to restore psychological content to painting. This was the coming of age of American art and had a great influence in Europe.

Action Painting incorporated existentialism to the extent that artists were asking questions like, Why are we here? Who is our higher power? What was I put on earth to do? None of this was representational in their work. In fact, having no imagery was the"in" thing.

Another twentieth century art movement called Minimalism got underway and took its foothold in the visual arts of painting and sculpture in the 1960s. The movement, begun in the U.S., developed because of an opposition to the Abstract Expressionism movement. Another battle of wills? This style of painting stressed the idea of reducing a work of art to the minimum number of colors, values, shapes, lines and textures. Artists like Barnett Newman, Agnes Martin, Ad Reinhardt, Ellsworth Kelly, Donald Judd, Sol Lewitt, Eva Hess and Frank Stella made little attempt to represent or symbolize in their art. However, they sometimes gave their works titles that allude to some degree of relationship with observed reality (i.e., Newman's "Stations of the Cross").

As we've seen, the artist's aesthetic point of view on color often requires both the psychological and psychophysiological information. Color aesthetic (according to Itten) has three aspects:

Impression, *which is visual*
Expression, *which is emotional*
Construction, *which is symbolic*

The next time you visit a museum, take a stroll around the different rooms and observe some of the work by the artists outlined in this chapter. You might discover something new in relation to your color preferences.

27

Chapter Three

Color
Wheel

History of the Color Wheel

Ever wonder how the color wheel came to be? Why twelve colors? What the sequence of color means? Well, let's explore the answers.

It seems to have started with scientist Sir Isaac Newton way back in 1666. He bent white light (sunlight) through a rectangular glass prism and voila! A spectrum of colors appeared. He then chose seven major colors and related them to the seven notes of a musical diatonic scale and to the seven planets. The musical connection is as follows: Red for C on the scale, orange for D, yellow for E, green equals F, Blue is G, indigo A and violet B. He then put these colors in a circle to form the first color wheel.

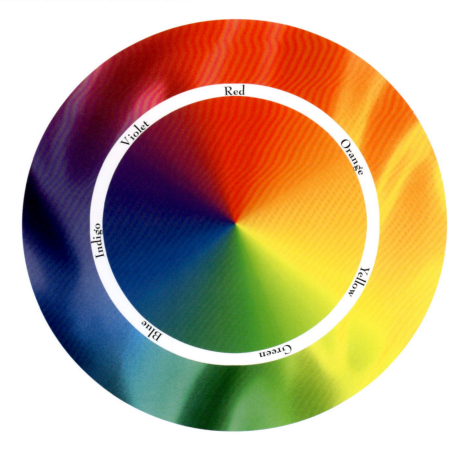

Evidently, Newton had a thing for the number seven. Indeed, he believed in numerology and thought that certain numbers governed all natural phenomena. When you think about it, it made sense for him to choose seven colors. After all, there are seven continents, seven seas, seven days in the week and a whole lot of other significant sevens to be sure. There are seven colors in the rainbow. Does this mean that Newton decided the colors of the rainbow? That's what they say.

How does a rainbow come to be? It occurs when light hits a cloud of water molecules and is refracted and reflected by the droplets, which act as a prism. Light hitting the right point of the water will be refracted by the outer surface and penetrate the water bouncing off the opposite side then refracts again as it reenters the air. Confusing? Think of a prism dangling in a window. Now read the first three sentences again. The various colors you see bouncing off the prism are caused by the above theory. The curve is a result of a 42-degree bend between the sun and us, due to the roundness of the earth.

Later, in the 1700's, primary colors (those that cannot be made from other colors—red, yellow, blue) were discovered as the fundamental nature of all other hues. In other words, all other colors are derived from these three colors. By mixing the primaries together in certain specific order, secondary colors (orange, green, purple) appeared.

Still later, another group of colors were "discovered" and tagged tertiary colors, which are a combination and compounding of the primaries and secondaries.

To get to the twelve colors in the current most popular color wheel, we have the three primaries with nine other colors spaced in between. The world doesn't exist by one color wheel

alone, though. There are others. One has as few as six while another has as many as thirty. The twelve colors in the wheel most used seem to be easiest to deal with for most design tasks.

So what about the sequence of the colors? First we have the primaries of red, blue and yellow. They are placed equidistant from each other in a triangular manner. Halfway between each primary and the next primary is a secondary color and on each side of the secondary color is a tertiary, a.k.a. intermediary color. Secondary colors as mentioned above are orange, green and violet. The intermediaries are red-orange, yellow-orange, yellow-green, blue-green, blue-violet and red-violet.

Thus we travel from red, the longest of light rays to violet, the shortest of light rays.

Another way to look at this color wheel business is to join the two ends of the color spectrum together and see that they form the color circle known as, you guessed it, the color wheel.

By the way, Johannes Itten produced the color wheel that is most recognizable today. Until the color wheel as we know it was established, others had their own color map. Goethe had a wheel and a triangle. Runge liked the triangle idea and added a solid color sphere. Blanc made up a six-point star; each point explored a different color.

Okay, so now we know how the color wheel was invented. Now, how are we supposed to use it? How does it work?

The first color scheme is the complementary color scheme. Complementary colors can be found on the color wheel by picking one color then seeing its complementary color exactly opposite it. For example, red is complemented by green. This complementary scheme pairs a cool color with a warm color.

What? Colors have a temperature? You betcha. Warm and cool: warm colors advance; cool colors recede. For the most part, red, yellow and orange are considered warm colors, while blue and green are considered cool colors. Want a cozy room, then use warm colors. Need to make a room appear larger, then use cool colors.

So what happens when you use cool and warm colors at the same time? Picture a plaid pattern of red, green, blue and beige. It works, doesn't it? Blue and green make a nice combination as does violet and green. A quality of richness seems to be present when warm and cool colors are blended in a pattern or a motif.

"It is better to look good than to feel good; you know what I mean? (You look mmmahvelous!)."
—Fernando

Next is the analogous color scheme. These are three colors that are next to each other on the color wheel. Look at the color wheel and see yellow followed by yellow-green followed by green. When using analogous colors, your décor will most likely be either warm or cool. If using overlapping analogous colors such as violet, red-violet and red, the use of the "odd" color as accent throughout the décor will spark things up well.

If there's a favorite color you want to use throughout the home, a monochromatic color scheme might be the best way to go. This scheme uses only one color but by adding either white or black to it, you produce various ranges of value to the initial hue.

There is also the triadic color scheme, which consists of three colors triangular to each other. An example would be red, blue, and yellow for a very vibrant color scheme. Another would be orange, green, violet, which can also be quite vibrant.

We're not done yet. We still have another set of combinations such as the split complementary color scheme. This one is made up of three colors also. For this you start with one color choice. Then go around the wheel and choose two colors that are on either side of the first choice's complementary color. Sound confusing? Go to the color wheel and see how this works. See red? Its complementary is green, right? Go to either side of the green and choose yellow-green and blue-green. And there you have it.

"All colors are the friends of their neighbors and the lovers of their opposites."
—Marc Chagall

CMYK AND RGB COLOR MODELS

CMYK identifies the four colors used in traditional printing presses and by graphic designers utilizing Adobe Photoshop and Quark XPress, and stands for, respectively, cyan, magenta, yellow and black. When these four inks/colors are combined, they can produce millions of different colors. CMYK is the standard color model used in offset printing for full-color documents.

In contrast, RGB refers to the so-called scientific hues, the additive primary colors red, green and blue, that, when mixed together in equal amounts create white light. Television sets and computer monitors display their pixels based on values of red, green and blue. In desktop publishing, converting the RGB colors into CMYK colors so that what gets printed looks the same as what appears on the monitor is a difficult task.

THE MUNSELL COLOR MODEL

The American artist Henry Munsell devised the Munsell Color System in 1898 as a way of specifying colors and showing relationships among colors in a "rational way." According to his system, every color has three aspects or qualities: hue, value and chroma. For each of these attributes, Munsell established numerical scales with visually uniform steps. In Munsell three-dimensional color space, hues are arranged in a circle, changing from red to yellow to green to blue to purple and back to red. As you move around the sphere, hues blend into one another continuously. Every discernable hue can be found on the hue circle. Value is the vertical axis changing from black at the bottom to white at the top. Chroma changes continuously from the neutral center to maximum saturation at the outer edge. In Munsell Color Space, each color occupies a single point, which can be described by its Munsell notation. Munsell's system is a universally accepted color system amongst printers and graphic designers.

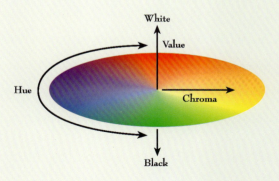

Hues, Tints, Shades, Tone
& Other Color Traits

When white is added to a particular color, or hue, it is referred to as a tint. Pastels are colors that have a lot of white in them. When black is added you get a shade. Tone pertains to the degree of brightness or intensity—how light or dark a color becomes when a hue is mixed with white or black.

Let's further clarify some color lingo:

Hue: *A color itself, as red or yellow.*

Tint: *A hue with white added.*

Shade: *A hue with black added.*

Tone or Tonal Value: *The comparative intensity of a color in contrast to white or black. It is possible to have many tones of the same hue.*

Value: *The relative amount of white or black in a color.*

Chroma: *A term used to designate the degree of intensity, brilliance, luminosity or saturation of a spectrum color. Yellow, near the center of the spectrum, is the most brilliant but has the least saturation and palest chroma. Red has a medium chroma; and blue, the darkest, with the greatest saturation.*

How can you use these color attributes in interior design? When should you use cool colors and when should you use warm colors? How about when warm and cool colors are used together? What's harmonious? What provides contrast? Read on.

Chapter Four

Color
Psychology

"When I'm not in my right mind, my left mind gets pretty crowded."

—Steven Wright

Everyone's psychological perception of color is subjectively different, but our biological base of color vision is typically universal, so there is commonness in color perception throughout the world. With that in mind, let's explore the various colors and their typical effect on our psyche.

Most of us will agree that red, yellow and orange are warm colors while blue, green and violets are felt as cool colors. But did you know that the brilliance, darkness and lightness of those colors could change the psychological meaning? Think of a pastel blue or a soft green and you will feel tranquil, even passive. Now picture an intense turquoise and see how you wake up your senses. Even though blue, which is in turquoise, has been known to lower blood pressure, bright turquoise will excite your visual perception.

Studies on color and the effect it produces in humans are often interesting. One such discovery is that your eyes will blink more frequently when exposed to the color red than to the color blue.

So how do colors feel and smell? How do they affect our moods and our taste buds? Let's explore the hues and their sometimes scientific and sometimes mysterious dominance over our minds.

Blue

Blue feels clean; it smells clean. Blue has many moods. It can be sad and depressing yet it also represents wisdom, trust and loyalty. It evokes feelings of hope, piety and spirituality. If we see blue on a food label we often associate it with lowered calories. Dairy products look inviting if blue is somewhere on the packaging. Though a blue tablecloth in a restaurant is good, not all blue in an eating environment will be appealing. Alfred Hitchcock had a rather different way of looking at things. Once he invited guests for a steak dinner. He changed all the light bulbs in the room to blue, which cast a grayish tint on the steaks rendering them so unappetizing that nobody ate and many guests actually got sick. In some studies, it's been noted that blue has an effect on the eyes, ears and nose, thereby affecting sight, sound and smell.

Blue has an effect on the eyes, ears, nose and throat, which interprets into sight, sound and smell. As the human eye matures, there is a preference, almost a need, for blue. This is due to the advancing of yellowing in the eye's lens. Blue, being the complementary color of yellow, supplies the needed hue to the yellowing eye. Another interesting observation is that in Western nations, blue is ranked as the favorite color in the spectrum.

Blue décor

What about a blue room? Designing in blue can be a challenge, yet the results can be quite enjoyable to live with. The challenge comes in knowing how to combine blue with other colors, and choosing the right shades of blue that will be personally pleasing. The White House has always had a blue room. There's something grand, majestic, yet calming about a room that is designed with the color blue. Think of the French Provincial style.

Blue can be used as a background color on walls and carpeting or it can be used as the foreground color in upholstery and draperies. Pleasant dreams might be the end result of coloring a bedroom in shades of blue. When in a blue environment, time seems to pass slowly and you don't feel rushed.

41

Red

Red feels exciting and smells exotic. It is associated with power, passion, dominance, activity and heat. It represents youthfulness, impulse and intensity. Red, and her softer, more compassionate sister Rose, is also a grounding color and can make you feel secure. It is associated with courtship and love. You've no doubt heard of "seeing the world through rose colored glasses," meaning that everything seems okay when viewed through these magic lenses. One medical study has revealed that chickens seeing red during the day are happier. There's even a company that markets red contact lenses for chickens! Supposedly, these rose colored glasses for chickens make them produce more eggs.

Then there's the evil twin of red, which can bring out rage, confrontation, fierceness, aggressiveness and bloody messes. But that bloodiness isn't always bad because red can be connected to life and living, which we automatically associate with life-blood. In Christianity, red stands for the blood of Christ. Red has been known to raise blood pressure. It also can cause people to lose track of time. In Casinos, red is widely used so that people will stay and continue to gamble, not realizing that time is flying by. Red stimulates appetites so it is often used in restaurants. Mending muscles have been known to heal quicker and feel better, if only psychologically, when exposed to red.

Red is said to affect motor skills. If you think about it, it makes sense emotionally. A shiny red car conjures up images of speed. Red is the prominent color of the Christmas season, which is full of hustle and bustle and lively parties. It is a color that demands attention. You see it in warning lights, fire engines and hydrants; it is associated with fire and flames. Red is the highest arc and outer edge of the rainbow and the longest wavelength of color.

Red décor

Red will wake up a room. It's the most dramatic color in the spectrum. It should be used as an accent in accessories, part of a pattern in upholstery or one impressive chair or bench. A touch of red is a good color to have in a nursery because it stimulates and aids the development of neural connections in an infant's brain.

Orange

Feels citrus-y, smells like orange. With that description, you'd think orange would be comfortable in its own skin, but it's not. Actually orange has an identity crisis. It is always in second place right after red. Orange is the natural color of fire but red is the name used to symbolize it. Orange represents excitement and can be stimulating. It can make you feel like hurrying and that is why it's usually a color used in fast food places and quick-mart type stores. They want you in and out of there quickly, so the smart store designers use orange to facilitate that.

Orange décor

Orange is good as an accent color coupled with brown or yellow. For use in a home, rust is the better shade to use, as it is easier on the eye.

Yellow

Yellow feels happy and smells like spring. It speeds metabolism so perhaps that's one reason it feels happy. But too much of a good thing can be bad. It's the most fatiguing color out there, especially pure, bright lemon yellow. Put a baby in a yellow room and s/he will cry more. Put adults in a bright yellow room and they will lose their temper after a while. A yellow kitchen might look bright and cheerful, but be assured that there will be more arguing between cooks in this atmosphere. I imagine, too, that movie stars throw more tantrums in yellow dressing rooms.

Yellow should be treated like sunlight. You want it around for the happiness it produces but you don't want it to be overpowering. Soft yellow is pleasing. Bold yellow should be used as an accent. Other attributes include philosophical detachment, anticipation, hope and communication. It expresses activity and in some religions is associated with the deity.

The first color the human eye will notice is yellow, hence the yellow yield signs, yellow fire engines and yellow caution lights. Are we contradicting ourselves? Didn't we say earlier that red was the first color we see? Red has the longest rays and therefore reaches our vision quickest, but yellow is the one that catches our attention first. Yellow is also said to be a color that is admired by intellectuals, perhaps because is stimulates the memory. It is associated with enlightenment, both mental and spiritual. A touch of yellow in every room might help in remembering where you left your keys, eyeglasses or the neighbor's phone number.

Yellow décor

Yellow does well watered down greatly with white for walls. If a room receives little or no sunlight, the soft yellow walls help make the room bright. Yellow sings arias as a splash of accent in pillows, vases and other accessories. Yes, one grand chair or sofa upholstered in yellow and piped in blue can be smashing. It's also a good color for a game room, study or office because it helps to keep you attentive. A yellow bathroom will take the chill out of the air.

Green

Green feels like nature and smells like nature. It reminds us of spring and, therefore, new beginnings. This is the most universal color because it represents trees and grass, which are predominant all around the world. It is commonly known and accepted as a color of peace and tranquility. Most everyone feels comfortable surrounded by green. It also signifies life, youth, hope and vigor. It can represent immortality and wealth.

Green is associated with throat healing. Someone concentrating on vocal skills or a new language is often attracted and feels better in a green environment. There is always a "green room" in theatres of performing arts where performers wait for their cue before going on stage. Because green is a color of peace and tranquility, it's no wonder that actors, musicians and the like can benefit from the "green room." It's a place where they can gather their thoughts and feel calm before a performance.

Design Tip
Start with a color you like, whether it's a bold, dominant color or a subtle neutral, and build around it.

Still on that diet? Green is good because it can help control the anxiety associated with the discipline required in controlling yourself from impulsive eating. Green is the most restful color to the eye; it has healing power and can soothe pain. If your work environment is saturated with green, it's been proven that you will have fewer stomachaches. And when the London Blackfriar Bridge was painted green, the suicide incidents dropped by 34 percent.

On the negative side, green is associated with poison. It is the color of mold, sickness and decay. It is also the color identified with envy, jealousy and superstition. Other negative connotations of green include drab military fatigues, prison walls, hospital greens, air and seasickness, slimy green insects, snakes and other icky green things associated with childhood.

Green décor

Lots of healthy green plants in any setting are always welcome. Green also does well as the dominant color in a scheme such as dark green wallpaper with green and red upholstery. In places with long winters, like New England and Scandinavia, a green wall can do wonders. It is another good color choice for studies and home offices, where getting down to business is important. Try a mint green bathroom for a soothing environment.

Purple

Purple has a velvety and royal feel and smells rich. This color stands for luxury, dignity, wealth and sophistication. It has magic, imagination and romance in its psychology. It also has a mystic quality to it and perhaps from that mysticism comes purple's not-so-great side of loneliness and mourning.

Purple has many faces. It is dignified, yet pompous. It is exclusive, yet conceited. Purple is the color of anger, divinity and royalty. It demonstrates authority, prestige and distance. Purple is intimately connected to intuition. Purple has the shortest wavelength and the fastest vibration in the color spectrum. If you are sick, do not wear purple as it enhances nausea.

Purple décor

Purple is an interesting color to decorate with. Pre-teens are usually thrilled to have their room done in purple or violet. Soft violet walls with white furniture and wispy white drapes can make a room really magical.

Doing an entire room in deep purple might be a bit overpowering, but it works really well as an accent. If a room is done primarily in blue, a splash of muted purple will bring a pleasant blend of color and a sense of depth to the room. Purple is a great companion for metallics. Adding a tinge of purple to a room is like adding a drop of Cajun sauce to a recipe. It's sure to spice up the place.

White

White feels pure, but has no scent. This color represents light, spirituality, hope, holiness, innocence, purity, cleanliness and goodness. White can awaken greater creativity. Other than to signify mourning in the Far East, there really is no negative side to white, at least psychologically speaking.

If you go by the book, white is not a color; it's an absence of color. In terms of light, however, white contains all color.

White conjures up images of billowy clouds, snow-capped mountains and luxurious wedding gowns. It can also be associated with ghosts and utter stillness. If you are a person who likes white, you are most likely a neat freak.

White décor

Of all the hues, the most romantic one to decorate with is white. Lacy or fluffy white bedrooms inspire sweet dreams and are reminiscent of a storybook

scene. White carpet, white walls, soft white sheers on the windows and a white bedspread make a great ambience. Add to that a large white paddle fan on the ceiling and a large wicker fan to hang on the wall in a natural finish and there you have it. Instant romance.

Creating an all-white room takes some courage, but the results can be so stunning that it's worth the anguish. An entire house can be done in white with tan and wood tones as accents. The feeling is fresh and new. However, if white is used extensively, without any relief, it can make a room or home feel completely cold and sterile. In decorating with white, which white you choose has a lot to do with the success of this venture. Also, white can be used with confidence if the right materials are used along with common sense fabrics and furnishings. Adding interest to a neutral scheme is key.

Black

Black feels ominous, smells like fear. This is possibly the most controversial of colors because it is connected with demons, yet it symbolizes stability and reliability. It is the color of mourning and despair, but also represents strength and authority. Black can feel sleek and sophisticated or heavy and enigmatic. Black is a protective color as well.

If you are a person who likes black you are probably fairly conventional and conservative. You may also be sophisticated and sexy and give an air of mystery. Prestige is no doubt high on your list.

Black décor

Black is seen as the opposite of white. It is a difficult color to use in décor because of its negative connotations and being linked to evil. Black coupled with gold accents can be very dramatic and opulent in a room

setting. Black and white is very contemporary while black and tan is considered more sophisticated. Take care when combining black with other colors, as it does not always interact well.

Psychology Behind Some National Flags

Why red, white and blue for the flag of the United States? Revolutionary times started it with red symbolizing valor and courage of the American people. White is for purity and blue implies honesty and peace.

Mexicans have green in their flag to represent independence, white for purity and red, which symbolizes union.

The Argentinean flag was born at an historical event. Blue and white badges were distributed at a political rally. It was raining heavily and the sky was very gray, then the sun shone through and its bright yellow was taken as a good omen, hence the blue, white and yellow flag.

"For in the end, we will conserve only what we love. We will love only what we understand. We will understand only what we are taught."

—Baba Dioum

Why is the Greek flag blue and white? Simple. The blue is a reflection of blue of the Greek sky and the white of the sometimes-billowing clouds you see up there. Or if you listen to another myth, Aphrodite is said to have flowed out of the turbulent Greek waves, which are also white.

49

The red in the Egyptian flag symbolizes the time before the 1952 revolution, deposing King Farouk and bringing the army to power. The white in her flag refers to the approaching revolution in 1952, which was carried out without bloodshed and ended the longtime monarchy. The color black in the flag represents the end of the oppression by the monarchy and British colonialism.

The flag of Guyana has FIVE colors that all mean something: Green stands for the nature that abounds in the country; white the rivers and water; gold in the arrow symbolizes Guyana's mineral wealth; black represents endurance of the people; and red the passion and determination of this young country to build a functioning nation.

The French flag was introduced in 1789 during the French revolution. The order of the colors at that time was red, white and blue. In 1830 the colors changed to blue, white and red. It is said that King Louis XVI wore a cockade of red, white and blue—the red and blue being the colors of the arms of the city of Paris and white the color of the House of Bourbon.

The Republic of Angola's national flag consists of two colors in horizontal bands. The upper band is bright red, representing the bloodshed by Angolans during colonial oppression, the national liberation struggle and the defense of the country. The lower one is black and represents the African continent. In the center lies part of a cogwheel, symbolizing the workers and industrial production; a machete symbolizing the peasants, agricultural production and the armed struggle; and a star, symbolizing international solidarity and progress. The yellow of these elements signifies the country's wealth.

Psychology aside, the colors of flags around the world is really a fascinating history lesson!

Psychology of Colors in Mourning

Blue: Mexico and some parts of Germany—represents heaven to which the soul is hopefully going. Blue is also the color of mourning in Syria and Iran.

Black: in the West—from the Victorian age when Queen Victoria wore only black after her husband died.
The ancient Egyptians and Romans also used black for mourning.

Red is the color of mourning in South Africa and it is also the color of mourning for a deceased Pope. In Thailand, a widow mourning her husband's death wears purple.

Yellow is the color of mourning in modern Egypt and Burma.

White means mourning in both China and Japan—represents purity and regeneration of the spirit.

What Your Choice of Color Says About You

Psychologists maintain that geographical location, religion and socioeconomic background determine color preferences. They theorize that the extroverted personality prefers the warmer, more vibrant colors while the introverted person is drawn to cooler, subtler tones. The Swiss psychologist, Max Luscher, who devoted his life to the study of how color affects behavior, developed a psychological and physiological test back in 1947 that can be self-administered.

Here's a simplified, short version of the test for you to try. Be spontaneous, and may the best color win!

Set yourself up with eight colored paint chips or pieces of colored paper. You'll need orange/red, blue, green, yellow, violet, brown, gray and black. Arrange them in a row—from left to right or top to bottom—in order of personal preference. Make note of the sequence in which you placed them. The left or top one should be the color you favor the most followed by your second choice and so on. After seeing the results, mix them up and try it again. Make note of your second set of choices. The reason for doing it twice is because not only are human beings complex, but it takes two tests to get a more overall picture of your feelings, making the second set of colors more valid than the first, according to Luscher.

You'll end up with a list of eight color preferences, corresponding to your most appealing to your least appealing color. The first six positions are the positives; the last two indicate the opposite or negative aspect of the colors.

The significance of the eight positions:

Position one is the color you prefer most and represents what you are seeking to achieve or a state of being you would like to attain. Position eight is the color you least prefer and represents something that you are seeking to avoid or something you are avoiding.

According to the eight Luscher colors, blue, green, orange/red and yellow are the "psychological primaries" and have special significance. The remaining four—violet, brown, black and gray are auxiliary colors. If you chose black, gray or brown in the first position, you may have a negative tendency toward life.

Interpretations for the colors are as follows:

Blue—Peace, loyalty—likes a calm and uncluttered environment

Green—Tenacity, strong-willed—can indicate an activist and/or a need to be acknowledged

Orange/Red—Activity, aggressiveness—may be bossy or an overachiever, lives life to the fullest

Yellow—Radiance, release—embraces the new, looks to the future, is hopeful

Brown—Substantiality, warmth—seeks security

Violet—Sexuality, high intensity—stresses wish fulfillment and a desire to achieve "magical" relationships

Gray—Subdued, non-committal—does not relish personal involvement

"Originality is simply a pair of fresh eyes."
—Thomas Higginson

Black—Authoritative, deep—repudiates things as they are, may act unwisely in a revolt against the status quo

An accurate and responsible interpretation depends largely on the where the placement of a certain color is in your eight color choices. For instance, where yellow in the first position shows a strong desire to escape from existing problems and remain ever hopeful, yellow in the sixth, seventh or eighth position may mean that hopes have been dashed so many times that a feeling of disheartenment and isolation exists.

Here's a further example of how the placement of colors comes into play. Suppose that blue appears as the first choice. This could indicate a basically quiet personality. Blue in the last position may imply some anxiety about loyalty. Blue in the third or fourth position indicates a state of tranquility while blue in the fifth position suggests an indifference to the color's symbolic meaning. Get the idea? Now you can interpret your selection of colors and, with this knowledge, color your interiors to better fit your personality.

By the way, the Luscher color test has been widely recognized as a major diagnostic aid to psychologists and physicians in Europe since it was first presented in 1947 at the International Congress of Psychology in Lausanne, Switzerland. The complete Luscher Test contained seven different panels of color (seventy-three color swatches) and required forty-three selections to be made. For this test, you'll have to consult a trained psychologist!

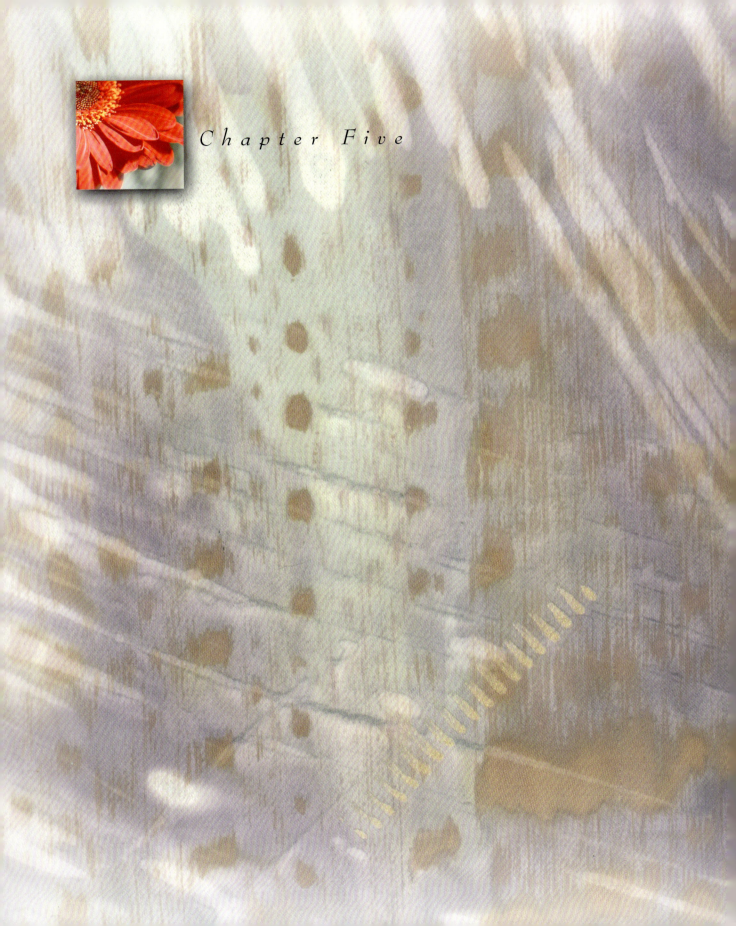

Chapter Five

Color
Healing

Color Energy

Color is all around so it's not surprising that it has an effect on every cell in your body. Sometimes color has such a subtle effect that you seldom give it a second thought. The effects of color on your moods, well being and approach to life are an ongoing interest to scientists and alternative health practitioners all over the world. The reason you like some colors more than others may be connected to the way they make you feel when you look at them or are surrounded by them.

Our most important energy source is light, and because the whole spectrum of colors is derived from light, our bodies absorb color energy. It's actually the photoreceptors in the retina, called cones, which translate this energy into colors. The retina contains three of these cones: one for blue, one for green and one for red. We perceive other colors by combining these colors.

When the energy of color enters your body, it stimulates the pituitary and pineal glands and triggers hormone production. This in turn influences your entire complex biochemical system and physiological processes.

Color Therapy *(Also know as chromotherapy)*

Color has often been connected with the art of healing. The use of color as a therapy has a long history and today color therapists abound. In the past, cures included the use of color through gems, body decoration, wraps or colored cloths on injured areas, and medicines made of dyes from animals and plants. The ancient Egyptians and Greeks built healing temples of light and color.

The Greek philosopher and mathematician, Pythagoras, is said to have cured disease through music, poetry and colored stones. Celsus, a Roman physician, prescribed medicines using white or purple violets, lilies, irises, roses and other color related plants.

Does color heal? Apparently, research has begun to substantiate the importance of color in treating disease and illness. A practitioner trained in color therapy employs color to balance energy in the body. An attraction to particular colors may indicate areas of imbalance in a person. Color therapists identify orange as a color that can stimulate the immune system and reduce pain. It has also been used as a healing agent for the treatment of ulcers and is considered to be very useful when fighting both depression and alcoholism.

"To live a creative life, we must lose our fear of being wrong."
—Joseph Chilton Pearce

Illnesses are sometimes diagnosed by observing changes in skin color: yellow may indicate a disorder of the liver, white a possible malfunction of the spleen. Observations made in clinical studies revealed that children with specific ailments sought out a playroom colored area that correlated with their ailment. Those with mending muscles chose red spaces. Those with throat problems were drawn toward green and blue areas.

"Color is a frequency that we resonate to sympathetically, or because we need more or less of it," says Leslie Moed, a healer who uses color. "It is not that color is negative; it's that if we have too much or too little of it, certain reactions are stimulated with it, depending on our make-up."

If you believe that color has the power to heal or bring about changes in your mental and physical well being, then the colors you select for your home may affect your life more than you think, as there is more to color than meets the eye.

Let's take a further look at some of the attributes of specific colors in relation to how practitioners and color therapists use color to help alleviate physical illnesses.

Red is the color of primal energy. The rays of this color can increase body temperature thereby producing heat, which vitalizes and energizes the body. Red is a stimulating color. Its presence can increase hormonal and sexual activity. No wonder it's thought of as the sexiest color. It's even been used to remedy impotence. Color therapists also use red to counteract anemia, low blood pressure and lack of energy. But watch out, too much red might produce a fever or leave you exhausted, and it can actually worsen certain conditions.

Orange, an optimistic color, is often used to treat melancholy. It has a sunny disposition naturally because it's the color of the setting sun. Orange can stimulate the appetite and immune system and reduce pain. Orange is uplifting and positive, but too much orange could adversely affect your nerves, especially if you are feeling stressed or you are quick to upset.

Yellow stimulates your mental energy and activity. It is the color of sunflowers and golden apples. It is also used to combat depression. It is effective in treating digestive problems, headaches, rheumatism and arthritis. It is also a color that can create or indicate anxiety and mental tension, so too much exposure to yellow might make you hyperactive, particularly if you're already prone to worrying a lot.

Green is the color of nature. The sight of green is undeniably associated with the smell of trees, grass and fields of greens. It is calming, both physically and mentally, so it is soothing to the nervous system, and a great healer. Green is the color of balance and harmony. Color therapists use green in treating people with cardiac conditions and high blood pressure. It is good for fighting fatigue. Cancer patients or people with any malignant tumor should stay away from green because it so inherently helps things to grow.

Blue is soothing and comforting. Its calming effect conjures up images of tranquility—the deep clear waters of the Mediterranean and mesmerizing blue skies. No wonder practitioners recommend it for curing insomnia. But if you have trouble getting out of bed in the morning, don't paint your walls blue. However, try blue if you're claustrophobic because this color gives an illusion of space. Physiologically, seeing blue reduces your blood pressure and respiration rate. Color practitioners use blue to reduce tumors, fevers and infections. Some doctors today use blue light to alleviate jaundice in infants. In color therapy, turquoise is used to combat inflammatory diseases and boost the immune system.

Indigo and the deeper shades of blue purify the blood stream and may help to reduce or stop excessive bleeding. It also is known to strengthen the lymph system, the glands and the immune system. Indigo blue is associated with the night sky—that dusky twilight before night falls. Therefore it is contemplative and can rouse one's devotion and intuition. Indigo is used to treat the eyes, ears, nose, mouth and sinuses.

Violet, also known as purple, is closely associated with meditation. It is cleansing on both the physical and spiritual levels. It is said that violet can be effective in treating cancer, arthritis and nervous disorders. It is a powerful healer.

Magenta is the most spiritual color. It is an agent for change and a good emotional stabilizer. If you have a problem "letting go," then this is the color for you.

Colors of the Chakra

The body contains seven major energy centers or chakra. In yoga, these are the power centers through which primal energy, or white light from the sun, is drawn into the body by our aura to nurture and support our very being. The seven chakra are located at various points of the body, from the base of the spine to the top of the head. It should come as no surprise that colors are associated with the body's chakra.

In order to balance your energy points with color you must first assess if your energy center points are balanced or unbalanced. An underactive chakra is usually one in which the energy is blocked, causing a lack of energy to perform daily functions. An application of color can help to stimulate the chakra into a balanced state. An overactive chakra may mean that there's too much energy flowing through the center, so an application of the complementary color is used.

The **root or base chakra** is red and governs the kidneys, adrenal glands, spinal column, colon, legs and bones. It awakens our physical life force.

The **sacral chakra** is located a few inches above the base of the spine and governs the reproductive system. You can stimulate this power center by visualizing orange, the color associated with it.

The **solar plexus chakra** is located on the spine behind the naval and is the center of will, self-determination and personal power. When you have a "gut feeling," this is where it comes from. This chakra is associated with the color yellow and governs the digestive system, pancreas, spleen, adrenals, liver, gall bladder, nervous system and muscles.

"Adventure is not outside of man; it is within."

—David Grayson

The **heart chakra** is green and governs the heart and lungs as well as the thymus and circulatory system. This is the center of love and self-acceptance. In yoga and other alternative health disciplines and exercise programs, you can use this center to heal relationships and bring balance and forgiveness into your life.

The **throat chakra** correlates to the color blue and governs the throat and thyroid. It is located on the spine behind the throat, and its center is communication and expression.

The **brow chakra** is the center of wisdom. It's called the third eye chakra and is located behind the space between the eyebrows. It is associated with indigo and governs the pituitary gland, ears, eyes and nose.

The **crown chakra** is identified with violet or white. It is the center of understanding, knowledge and wisdom, and it governs the pineal gland, the brain and the central nervous system. The crown chakra is located at the top of the head.

> The general rule for the chakra: *If the chakra is underactive, an application of its basic color is used. If the chakra is overactive, the application of the complementary color is used.*

If you are still asking yourself, so what exactly is color energy? Simply put, through color we receive some energies we need to sustain a healthy mind, body and soul. If you pay attention to this when something goes wrong in your life, you just might find yourself relaxing in a bath of essential oils, healing with candles or eating more foods of a certain color. Color alone will not change your life, but it could be a fun start. Understanding why certain colors affect you favorably while others cause negative feelings can, it seems, help you along on your way to healing.

Feng Shui & Colors

Feng shui (pronounced *fung schway*) has been a buzzword in interior design for the past few years. Though it might seem like a fad at this juncture due to its popularity, the truth is that the art of feng shui design has been around for centuries. The words come from the Chinese, meaning *wind* and *water*, and the concept is based on the notion that every space has an invisible energy, also called *chi*, that flows

through and is affected by several factors. *Chi* needs to move freely, lingering perhaps here and there, but never stagnating. This free flow allows positive impact on the inhabitants while stagnant *chi* will cause negative effects.

How is this positive *chi* flow accomplished? Through many means including proper furniture placement and use of color. Sound hokey? Many Americans have adopted this ancient Chinese tradition not only in their homes but also in executive offices of large corporations, as it seems to work. Curious? Let's keep exploring the idea.

Feng shui design insists that everything, animate or inanimate, has energy and that is the key to understanding how to control the use of that energy. Still unclear? How about this example: *Chi* must flow through the home like a river. If the space is too open or linear, *chi* will flow in the front door and directly out the back. The opposite also comes into play. If the space has too many oddly placed walls or furnishing, the *chi* may become trapped and stagnate. Remember, chi needs to linger yet flow freely.

Feng shui works by balancing—moving, adjusting, arranging and adding certain objects, elements and colors to *even out* the flow of energy in the home or even one particular room. To balance the home with good *chi*, there are several techniques used. Let's take windows and doors, their placement in a room and what the *chi* is likely to do. If a window faces a door and there is no barrier between them, be it a chair, a tree or some other furnishing, the *chi* will flow in and right out again, depriving those who live there its energizing effect. But what if furniture or trees are not appropriate for the space? Window treatments will then be the answer. A honeycomb shade or a sheer drapery will allow the air to be trapped a bit and thereby help deflect *chi* to other areas of the room.

In addition to furniture placement and window treatments, there is also the element of color. Placing the right color in the right place is said to result in wondrous things. For example, if a family is constantly arguing, something green placed near the center of the left wall of the room might bring a truce. Are you looking for more wealth? Place something from the purple spectrum in the upper left hand corner of your workspace or home. Is romance lacking in your life? Put pink, red or white in the upper right hand corner of your family room or bedroom. Colors can be used via plants, flowers, pictures, upholstery and painted or wallpapered rooms. For intellectual enhancement, surround yourself with yellow. Soothing colors such as blues and greens promote better rest and relaxation.

There are several schools of feng shui thought. One of them (and the one mostly referred to here) is the Black Hat Sect of feng shui. It is this school of thought that is used in the U.S. more than any other school. At the heart of its practice is *chi* energy, and emphasis is on the best position for the space, not absolute direction as, say, with the Compass School.

Also fundamental to feng shui is the notion that our whole existence is founded upon five elements: earth, metal, water, wood and fire. Interesting, in light of the fact that back in

Chapter One we mentioned four of these elements in relation to the Greeks. Did they get a jumpstart on this feng shui notion or did the Chinese corner the market all along? Something to think about.

Each of the following elements is associated with certain qualities of our life and with specific colors.

Earth—yellow, brown and orange, signifies harmony, wholeness, stability and being grounded.

Metal—white gold and silver, is associated with children and leadership, money and success.

Water—black, blue and purple, is connected to power and wisdom as well as money and emotions.

Wood—green, has to do with family and good health, growth and expansion.

Fire—red, implies passion, wealth and energy, plus it has to do with fame and reputation.

Let's explore feng shui and colors a bit more:

Red—Lacquer your front door red and invite opportunity and fortune into your home.

Yellow—Paint your living room or den yellow and its positive energy will benefit everyone who comes there.

Orange—A few accents of burnt orange in a family room can ignite your creativity.

Design Tip

Hues that are similar in saturation and value can unify a room and make a space seem larger. Carrying the same colors throughout the room as well as into the adjacent rooms will open the spaces as well as bring a feeling of continuity to them.

Green—Introduce lots of plants and foliage into your environment and feel the sense of harmony it produces. Plants eat toxicity, so they have to be healthy to perform this function.

Blue—Decorate your home office with blue and watch your career flourish. Do you have a hyperactive child? Paint his or her bedroom blue.

Purple—A couple of lavender or mauve touches in a room is great for creating a space in which to meditate.

Magenta—A splash of magenta in your bedroom may get you to clean out your closets.

Chapter Six

Color
Properties

Color is produced *when light hits an object & then reflects back to the eye.*

Color is power. Color communicates. Color attracts. Color has force, weight, action and temperature. Now that's a lot for one element to do.

Regarding the first three elements of color described above, let me share a little poem with you written by Elizabeth Barrett Browning.

The Lady's Yes

'Yes,' I answered you last night;
'No,' this morning, 'sir I say'.
Colors seen by candle-light
Will not look the same by day.

Let's explore force, weight, action and temperature of color. Do the colors in a home reduce or increase energy consumption? Absolutely! Consider this. On a hot, sunny day, isn't it cooler to wear white than to wear black? Try standing in the hot, scorching sun dressed in black. It is a scientific fact; white reflects radiant energy while black absorbs it.

Let's take this principle home. A dark roof will attract energy rays from the sun. The dark roof then becomes hot, so the house under it will be warmer. To prove this, a test was conducted in Austin, Texas, resulting in the following statistics: a white roof had a temperature of 110 degrees F, an aluminum coated roof came in at 140 degrees F and a black roof showed a scorching temperature of 190 degrees F.

Granted, a well-ventilated attic with heavily insulated floor will stop much of the heat in summer and cold in winter from going into the house, but most homes are not well-insulated, particularly older homes.

Colors inside the home also have an effect on energy savings or consumption. Same principle applies. Dark walls absorb more light and reflect less light, hence the need for more electricity to be used to see well in a dark colored room. But if a color is preferred to a plain white wall, there is still a good solution. Most paint manufacturers will tell you the Light Reflectance Value (LRV) of any color paint chip. White reflects 80 percent of the light while black reflects 5 percent. With those numbers as comparisons, you can see that the higher the LRV number of the paint color, the better the light reflection will be and the less artificial light will be needed.

Besides the actual LRV, color also has a physiological effect. Blues and greens are considered cool colors. Tests document that people in a room that is colored in these hues will estimate the temperature to be 6 to 10 degrees warmer.

> *"Moonlight is sculpture."*
> —Nathaniel Hawthorne

Your best bet is to have a good combination of dark or at least intense colors with light, airy ones. If a dark wall is in order, surround it with light colored furniture, a light ceiling and three other walls of lighter color. Use warm colors in a room that has little or no direct sunlight and cool colors in a room that is saturated with sunrays.

73

Without light there is no color. With a little light there is perception of color but shaded. True color will not be visible until full light shines on it. Ms. Browning's lady figured that out the morning after. So now that we know that light is color, let's go on to the next elements of color: force and weight. How can color have force and weight? I don't know, but I can prove to you that it does. Shine a ray of light on a sensitively balanced scale and watch it tip in the direction of the light.

It seems the studies best known in the world of design are those that deal with and compare the light (color) of long wavelengths such as red and yellow to that of short wavelengths like green and blue. The action of color is its vibration; it is also its wavelength. Remember, red has the longest wavelength, while blue is on the short end. Red produces action in your bloodstream, blue calms the action in your veins. Red, orange and yellow are heating rays and they do produce heat while blue, violet and green are cooling. Okay, another experiment for you to try. Place a thermometer in a colored glass of water. Let strong light shine through it. You will see that a red colored glass gives off the most heat while blue rays from a blue glass produce the least amount of heat.

Color is capable of setting up "responsive vibrations" in more ways than meet the eye. Researchers in Russia proved this by using blind subjects. The subjects were given certain colors to touch. Red was described as warm, rough and tingling, while blue was described as smooth and cool even though the materials used were of the same temperature and texture.

All colors have three properties. When speaking of color attributes, or properties, we mean hue, saturation (also called chroma) and lightness (also called value). The hue is the name of the color (blue, for example), the characteristic by which one color is distinguished from another and is determined by wavelength. The saturation is the attribute by which a particular color is distinguished. Saturation (chroma) is often referred to as the strength of a color or its intensity or, if you will, how pure it is, which usually suggests that no other color has been added. Then there is lightness (value). This is the quality that distinguishes light color from dark color (light green, for example). The lightness of a pigment is measured by how much light is reflected from its surface.

Similar colors make the eye relax and combine space rather than divide it. If you want to create space in a room, use similar colors throughout rather than contrasting colors. Remember the art of pointillism discussed in the chapter on artists and their colors, where paintings were created in small dots of diversely colored pigments? This is where the brain blends the colors automatically in the involuntary process of optical mixing. It's the eye that does it, not the color itself.

"Okay, so what's the speed of dark?"
—Steven Wright

Actually, color only exists in our brain but it is the eye that sends it the message. Color is the result of different wavelengths of light, and those wavelengths stimulate certain parts of the brain. What is called the 'experience' of color is dependent upon the intensity of light. Other factors, such as how that light is reflected from the surface and the colors of other surrounding objects will determine the brain's interpretation of a particular color's *chroma* and *value*. Sounds complicated but actually all this means is that the object is reflecting the color that you see (blue, for example) and absorbing the colors that you don't see.

Here's an example of how the eye and brain 'make' color. Color originates in light. Sunlight, as we perceive it, is colorless but a rainbow is testimony to the fact that all colors of the spectrum are present in white light. Take a yellow lemon. All colors of sunlight shine on that lemon. The surface of the lemon absorbs all of those colored light rays, except for those that correspond to yellow. Yellow is then reflected to the human eye. Now that the eye has received the reflected yellow light, it sends the message to the brain and the brain says, "I see yellow." So, color is really an aspect of vision and visual perception. Interesting, huh?

Photobiology is a science that studies the interactions of light with living organisms. This science is yet another way to explain color, light and eye/brain connection in that it maintains that light interacts with cells in the retina of the eye so we can see. Photobiology goes beyond eyesight. It maintains that light is used to improve human health and includes phototherapy, which is the use of light to treat various conditions such as cancer, leukemia, jaundice and some skin conditions as discussed in Chapter Five.

Does light with all its colors have impact on how we live and how our bodies react? If we have any connection to the animal world, this little incident might shine light on that subject. To protect against vandalism, a zoo in Syracuse installed floodlights. The reported result goes like this. "The zoo has been turned into a veritable maternity ward. The cougars fell in love all over again and produced their fourth litter. We collected five goose eggs. At least eight lambs were born, and the deer population increased by twenty. Big Lizzie gave birth to a bear cub. The wallaby produced a new mini-kangaroo and the chimpanzee is expecting in August." To decipher this phenomenon, I can only surmise that the floodlights were to blame—they added light to make the "day" longer like springtime and all the animals became enamoured with one another once again.

Remember the discotheque scenes of the '60s and '70s with the flashing, flowing colored lights? The idea behind the light scene, coupled with the roaring music, was to block out the real world without the use of drugs. There was more to that idea than just a design concept. Flashing lights have been found to induce seizures of epilepsy. Strobe lights can be hypnotic. Minor forms of nervous breakdowns have occurred under these flashing, flowing colored light conditions.

Glare can be hazardous, too. Visual exposure to a snow-covered field can be uncomfortable, even painful to the eye and might even cause retinal injury. Many home interiors are painted in white or off white. Not a problem when blended and accented with other colors in upholstery, carpet, drapes and accessories. If those white or off white walls are highly illuminated either by sunlight or artificial light, the result could be bad for you. And too much white such as on ceiling, walls, floors and upholstery can cause eyestrain. If a white-on-white color scheme sounds appealing, use a wood floor with wood accessory tables and add

greenery around the room with trees and plants. Toss a few colored pillows on the sofa and love seat to cut the white and add interest and diversion to the eye. Put paintings on the wall that work well with those colored pillows.

How We Experience Color

The effects of color are vast and complex and take many years of study to understand, but some knowledge goes a long way in helping us color our surroundings in a manner that is pleasant and nourishing to live in. There are some color experts who state that there are six basic levels of how we experience color. The first is our biological reaction to a color stimulus. Life is governed by the radiation of the sun, which is visible light, and light is color. Plants get their green color from the pigment chlorophyll, which is used for photosynthesis. In somewhat the same way, we not only see color but we also absorb it. A pink light will make a person less aggressive even if he or she is blindfolded.

The second level is called collective unconscious. As per Carl Jung, the collective unconscious is part of our psyche that has nothing to do with conscious or unconscious reactions based on personal experience. It is more akin to instinct of predispositions of our species inherited from our ancestors. Our likes and dislikes of certain colors, therefore, come with birth just as our eyes and ears do. The development and further affinities toward certain colors then develop according to life experiences. If a child growing up in a very loving and nurturing family was surrounded by blue as the main color in the décor, as an adult, blue will be a favorite color and one that will

provide some form of love, albeit abstractly, but still supportively. Which melds us into the next level.

Third on the list is conscious symbolism and associations. There are learned responses such as the blue scenario above. There is a universal thought to this level. Most people in all cultures associate blue with sky and water, green with nature, red with revolution and gold with glamour or riches. This association is what makes us perceive a home as friendly, warm, cold, depressing and so on. This association though takes on a personal flavor according to life experiences. The person who loves blue due to childhood memories might be entertaining someone in their home who came from a background where blue provoked sadness. To one the home is nurturing, to the other it evokes sorrow.

Design Tip

Have you found the perfect sofa with the perfect fabric on it? Want it to stand out as the perfect piece that it is? Place it against a wall of contrasting color. Say the sofa is red leather. Put it against a yellow wall or a white wall. The sofa will stand out as if in a spotlight.

As humans, we receive 80 percent of our information from the environment. For example, the experience of new green growth in nature teaches us continuity, rebirth and therefore hope. As we mature and become more aware of the greatness of the universe, the association with green invokes, in some, powerful religious symbolism such as the spirit of hope represented by the Holy Spirit. Perhaps this is why green is always welcome in any décor particularly in the form of plants and trees. This takes us to the next level or color experience.

The fourth level deals with cultural influences. It has been proven that symbolism, impressions and even mannerisms characteristic of specific cultures play a role in how color is used. For example, turquoise is the national color in Persia. The reason for this is that in ancient times, Persians wore turquoise gems to ward off evil. The Japanese are attracted to the gentle colors of water, sky and wood. Indians prefer bold, vivid colors such as reds and yellows.

Color preference level number five deals with the influence of trends, fashions and styles. The first place color trends appear is in clothing fashion. Interior design and architecture change color after fashion color has taken hold. Everyone seems to get bored after a few years with one set of colors so in order to keep consumers consuming, color trends shift to create new interest. This is the level at which our interiors become dated such as the familiar olive green and harvest gold of the '70s and the mauve and teals of the '80s.

The sixth level deals with personal relationship to color. Sounds odd—"a personal relationship with color"—but it does exist. Everyone has likes, dislikes and indifferences towards certain colors and that is what makes it "personal." This sixth level is more or less a summary of the other five levels in that personal color preferences are influenced by trends, culture, color association, the collective unconscious and the biological reaction we all have toward color.

What does all this gibberish teach? The answer to this is that it is best to recognize personal color likes and dislikes then plan around those for the color motif of the home. Knowing why we have certain likes and dislikes sometimes helps in understanding how important it is to surround ourselves with the colors that will provide mental and physical comfort.

The point is that color has many faces. Some of our connotations and feelings for colors come from training, lifestyles and our heritage. But when it comes right down to it, the beauty of a color is truly in the eye of the beholder.

Chapter Seven

"Light is the symbol of truth."
—James Russel Lowell

The use of light in our homes is very important. Because light affects color, or hue, colors seem to shift when influenced by light and shade. Even the location of the sun, or a cloud going by, will change color from one minute to the next. The way light reflects the fabrics we choose will have a great effect on how that fabric will actually look and blend with other fabrics and colors in the room. It is good to note here that whenever you are changing or adding some fabric or carpet to your home, ask the salesperson if you might borrow a sample of it. Look at the sample in the room where it will be used and observe what it does at various times of the day, as well as in the evening, with artificial light. You might be surprised. What looks perfect in the store's light might not work at all in the light of your home. What about paint? Those tiny 1-inch by 2-inch samples will never give an accurate picture of a full wall painted that color. It might be worth the time, cost and effort to buy a small amount of the paint you intend to use and sample a portion of the wall with that paint. If it works, great; if it doesn't you can just paint over with the correct color (when you find it!) and nothing is lost.

Metamerism: *A scientific description of a common color phenomenon: two color samples that appear to match under one light source no longer match when viewed under a different light source.*

Color and light go hand in hand, or in the case of a client of mine, face to face. Before we refurbished her home, she had those old Hollywood lights around each and every bathroom mirror in the house. You've seen them. They are the round lamps that go up the sides and across the top of mirrors. This client couldn't figure out why she looked so much better in one bathroom mirror than she did in a different one, even though the lighting was exactly the same. When I looked into each of these bathrooms, I found the walls in one bathroom had a peach tone on them while the other bathroom was of a blue-gray color. It was the color that made the difference. The peach colored bathroom gave a nice warm glow to her complexion while the blue-gray color ashened her face. The light, being bright, made the colors reflected from the mirror more intense and that reflection bounced right off the mirror and onto her face. It is good practice to use amber lights in restaurants and lounges because everyone looks more attractive under that color. It should be the color of light used in powder rooms where bright task lighting isn't needed. Then all users of that restroom will look good.

Background colors do have a big effect on what our brain interprets the foreground color to be. To prove this point, take a bright red fabric and put it on top of a bright green fabric. The red will appear very red. Take that same red fabric and place it on top of an orange fabric and the red will not seem as brilliant. Once again, we see that color is relative. When light shines on these colors, their effect is even more intense, and the greater the light, the greater the contrast or lack thereof will be seen.

For the rest of the house, the type of lighting will depend on the intensity of it. If we want to imitate natural light we need to realize that it (natural light) varies from morning to noon and then to evening with a variety of colors from pink, orange and yellow to white and blue and back to the pinks and oranges at sunset. If a room is to have a low level of illumination, it is best to use warm colored lights. If the room will have high levels of light, such as task areas, cooler light is needed to assure a more normal appearance to the skin as well as to be able to see what you're doing.

Sunlight and artificial light usually work as a tag team, one picking up where the other leaves off. But then sometimes there's not enough sunlight or too much of it coming into a

room. If a room is on the dark side due to lack of sunlight, a cure would be to use light colors in the room, particularly on the floor, walls and ceiling. The color used on these surfaces should reflect as much light as possible, thereby taking advantage of any stream of light entering the room. On the floor, for example, a glossy light colored tile will do a great job of reflecting light. The wall farthest from the window or the wall that receives the least amount of light should be treated with something reflective. A mirror would work, if it were appropriate for that space. Faux paint or wallpaper with reflective qualities in it would also work. Another trick is to add a fluorescent cornice light from end to end on that darkest wall. The cornice will add light and also enhance the colors and textures on the wall as well as furniture and fabrics in close proximity to that illuminated wall. Pale colors reflect light, while dark colors absorb it.

If a room is overpowered with sunlight, sheer draperies can cut the glare while still letting the sun brighten the room. The color chosen for the sheers will wash the room in that color, particularly when the sun is pouring in the most. If a cream colored sheer is selected, the room will have a vanilla glow to it. An intense color on the drapery could result in an eerie look or at best, a distracting one, so careful selection of fabric color is imperative. If the sun is still too powerful for comfort in the room, the far wall can be painted a dark color. It will not only cozy up the room but will also add drama. Keep in mind that a floor receives most of the sunlight entering a room. To reduce the amount of sunlight in a room, a dark floor should be chosen, such a stained wood, adobe tile or deep colored carpet.

One of the hardest parts of deciding the right color of paint for a room is getting a grip on how it will respond in different lighting situations. The reflective quality of paint will have a great bearing on the lightness or

86

darkness that will be perceived in a room. As discussed in Chapter Six, paint companies, such as Porter Paints, have formulas for their paints that tell what the Light Reflectance Value (LRV) is on any or their paints. The percentage tells you the amount of light thrown back. For example, an 80 percent reflection will give back a lot of light, while a 15 percent reflection will absorb most of the light and give back little.

When the sun goes down and artificial light takes over, the principles are a little different. The sun will come in from the window or windows while the artificial light is usually from the ceiling, wall, floor or table lamps. The room that didn't get much sunlight during the day should be colored in a light tone, if the above suggestions are used, so the room will feel as though it were better lit during the day. Lamps at end tables and by a reading chair will make those light tones glow in the evening. In the case of the room overpowered by sunlight in the day, we've darkened the area with paint, floor covering and fabrics that will now need to be lightened. Two ideas come to mind. One is to leave the room in a darkened state to create a warm and intimate atmosphere. Such can be the case in a room that is used mostly for television viewing with little reading or tasking going on. The other is to illuminate well with properly placed lighting. The reflective quality of the paint will again be a

"Different colors can receive from the same shadow an equal degree of darkness. It is possible for colors of all sorts to be transformed, by a given shadow, into the color of this shadow."

—Leonardo da Vinci

factor. If the paint has sheen to it, it will reflect more of the light. A sateen or chintz fabric, even darkly colored ones will also reflect more light than a dull or nubby fabric.

Color, light and space can all work together to make a not-so-perfect room more appealing. If space is something that needs to be visually expanded try this on for size. Small, square rooms will do well if two opposite walls are painted the same color, preferably an intense one. The deep color will create a feeling of depth, therefore opening up the room. A deep, deep ocean is seen as dark water. The feeling of depth and great expanse is there even though the water is right there where we can touch it.

Another solution to small rooms is the use of gray or blue-gray as background colors. This gray influence makes other colors look better. Gray or blue gray colors lend themselves well as backdrops for almost any scene. All other colors used in a room with gray background will stand out.

If a room is very spacious, and you like bold, bright colors, you have a winning combination. An example would be to use bright yellow and intense blue for a color scheme. The room will come out looking cheery and fun, and the intensity and boldness of the colors will cozy up an otherwise sprawling atmosphere.

Have we shed enough light on this subject? If not, perhaps the descriptions below will help when lighting your interiors.

Various Types of Lighting
(All Affect Color Appearance)

Ambient: A hidden source of light that washes a room aglow. Flattens an interior and creates very little shadow. A wall sconce is an example of ambient lighting. So are those Japanese paper shades you find in stores. Use of a dimmer can provide ambient light.

Accent: Directional lighting or lighting that adds interest or highlights a certain object or unusual architectural feature in a room. A bulb and some kind of shield to direct the light are all that's needed for this type of lighting. Halogen spotlights and table lamps with opaque shades are good ways to achieve accent lighting.

Task: Task lighting is just that—lighting that's used to perform our daily activities—reading, cooking, shaving, putting on make-up are examples. Needs to be glare-free. Effective task lighting enhances visual clarity and keeps the eyes from getting tired. Different banks of light are useful in the kitchen—near the stove and chopping areas are places for this type of lighting. Task lighting sources are never seen and any task light should have a reflective shield. Ambient lighting and task lighting go hand in hand. Pools of light created by several spots produce a lovely effect.

Aesthetic: Lighting itself can be a work of art. A neon sculpture would be purely decorative and an example of aesthetic lighting. A spotlight illuminating a statue on a pedestal or portrait on the wall is also artistic. This type of lighting needs to be used along with other lighting types.

Natural: Sunlight, candlelight and firelight. This is light that moves and is sometimes referred to as kinetic. The quality of natural light, sunlight in particular, depends on many things—time of day, weather, what season it is. Fall has a different light than summer, for instance. The setting sun gives a different kind of light than midday sun. This is lighting we have little control over.

Various Types of Bulbs
and What They Do

Tungsten: Gives off a slightly yellow tinge. These are your ordinary light bulbs.

Spotlight: Gives focused bursts of white light.

Halogen: Gives the closest approximation of natural daylight, known as "white light." Colors appear sharper under halogen light. The halogen bulb is also an energy saver. Can be dimmed.

Fluorescent: Has a green or pink color value. The typical fluorescent gives a flat, cold light, often bluish and harsh. Also daylight-equivalent but cannot be put on a dimmer. There are many types of fluorescents on the market today—warm ones, cool ones and specially colored ones.

Incandescent: Refers to several types of bulbs, including halogen and some fluorescents. This type of light has a warm quality and is very complimentary to skin tones and psychologically appealing. It's an inviting light.

What's the Best Light to Use?

There are many ways to light a room. The room's function greatly determines the way it should be lit. Here are some examples.

If a room is too tall, use low luminaries that let no light out the top to help shorten the gangling aspect of those high ceilings.

If a room is too small, visually push one wall open by washing it with light.

If a room is too wide, illuminate the narrow ends.

If a room is to narrow, illuminate the wide sides.

Rooms should be illuminated to accommodate the user's needs. So what about a multi-purpose room? You will need to divide it up into activity areas. If there is a dining room table or game table, a separate light hanging over the table will be necessary. A reading chair in the same room will need a lamp that directs light over the shoulder of the reader, being careful not to place the source of light behind the person's head so as to avoid shadows on the book or magazine.

Design Tip

To correct a room that is too long and narrow, use light colors on the long walls and a dark color or dark furniture on the short wall. A very intense color on the short wall will do the same trick.

Dark walls and floors reflect less light than light colored ones. If you're looking for an intimate atmosphere, use little illumination in this kind of dark room. On the other hand, be aware that this darker room will require more light for general tasks.

A balancing act is important in all rooms when it comes to light. An evenly lit room will become boring rather quickly. It will also tend to fatigue the user, particularly if repetitious tasks are being performed. Up lights, down lights and wall washers work well together. They make a good team in almost any room, and if dimmers are added, they can perform well in any atmosphere.

Chapter Eight

Color
Discovery

"I am white, I am black, I am yellow, I am brown . . . There is nothing wrong with this reality. In order to make harmony between peoples, the basis is diversity. It is from different types and different races that harmony may come."

—Dalai Lama

Have you ever wanted to have your bedroom ceiling painted blue with some fluffy white clouds in it? Perhaps it's because you spent some time as a child looking at the sky and identifying shapes and forms with a friend or relative. As you've discovered already, fond memories often stick in our minds in the form of color.

White is often used to depict peppermint because white always meant fresh for as long as we can remember.

Anyone out there like chocolate? Brown on candy wrappers has been known to stimulate the taste buds and produce saliva—yes, drooling in some cases!

We know that when the traffic light turns red we stop and when it turns green we go. This mental process is instant and comes from memory.

Have you ever had a strong emotional reaction to a color? If perchance you've experienced seeing the clear turquoise waters of the Caribbean and the way it helps to

soothe away tension and stress, then indeed you have. Maybe you'd like to recreate that feeling—capture the mood. Who wouldn't? Or possibly you've walked into a space that's primarily done in red and the passion to dance arose within you. That too would be considered a powerful response to color.

You can also connect with color through what is called "guided imagery," a technique developed by Leatrice Eiseman and mentioned in her book titled *Colors for Your Every Mood*. Here's how. Let your mind wander. Where does it take you? Do you imagine sitting under a redwood tree in northern California? Are you transported back in time to your grandmother's porch looking out over a cool mountain stream? Perhaps your fondest memories are of snow-capped mountains, sandy beaches or autumn foliage. Whatever they are, why not use these remembrances and the colors associated with them to inspire your color preferences in the home?

Still in doubt about color? To help you with discovering your ideal colors, take the following color association quiz. Choose from the categories of warm, cool or neutral colors. Ask yourself what color you would like to put on or be surrounded by as you make each choice.

Warm Colors: Yellow, red and orange—and colors next to them on the color wheel

Cool Colors: Blue, green and purple—and colors next to them on the color wheel

Neutral Colors: Black, gray, white, brown, and beige—not on the color wheel

Activity	Color Choice	Warm	Cool	Neutral
Taking a bath				
Working out				
Preparing a meal				
Taking a walk				
Listening to music				
Reading a book				
Playing a board game				
Writing a letter				
Doing a chore				
Surfing the net				
Taking a nap				
Engaging in a phone conversation				
Celebrating a special occasion				
Painting a picture				
Shopping for a gift				
Riding in a car				
Trying on clothes in a store dressing room				
Eating in a fancy restaurant				
Buying groceries				
Performing in front of an audience				
Dancing with a loved one				
Meditating				
Gardening				
Sitting in your favorite chair sipping wine				
Waking up on a weekend morning				
Eating breakfast				
Watching television				
Enjoying conversation with friends				
Playing with children				
Caring for someone in need				
Total				

What to Do Next

Tally up separately the number of warm, cool and neutral colors you picked. Then use the following information to use color to your benefit wherever you choose in your home.

What Your Color Choices
Say About You

Warm colors advance. If you picked mostly warm colors, you are probably daring and full of life because these colors are active and stimulating. You seek success and stimulation and desire to live life to the fullest. You are active and outgoing, sometimes even restless. You are also volatile and need to feel that events are developing along desired lines. You are usually ready and willing to participate in things of excitement or stimulation and you can be very sensuous.

Cool colors recede. If you picked mostly cool colors, then you are apt to be quite contemplative by nature, as these colors are serene and calming. You are probably very orderly, methodical and self-contained. You need to be respected, recognized and understood by those close to you. You will act with calm in most situations in order to handle an existing relationship. You like to feel relaxed and at ease with your associates and those close to you.

Neutrals? You might be cautious and sophisticated, but a down-to-earth type person. You aren't easily satisfied with life. You often need peace and quiet and at the same time require secure relationships. You often have an unsatisfied need to associate yourself with others whose standards are as high as yours. You need to be loved and admired for yourself. You often require

99

the attention and recognition and esteem of others. You feel that life has much to offer and must be experienced to the fullest. As a result you will pursue your objectives with a fierce intensity and will not let go of things. You feel most at peace when you have finally reached your goal.

What to Do if You Haven't a Clue?
Have Your Colors Done on You!

About fifty years ago, Suzanne Caygill developed a system to determine a person's best colors according to skin, hair and eye pigmentation. Around the same time, Gerrie Pinckney and her partner, Marge Swenson, expanded that theory connecting a person's color preference with the four seasons, then wrote a book about it, which is now out of print. Autumn, for example, is rich in rusts and golden tones so wearing these hues will enhance an autumn-type person's beauty. Take it a step further and we discover that the same person looks good surrounded by intricate patterns such as paisley and plaid. Carole Jackson popularized this theory in her book, *Color Me Beautiful*, which is still available.

Stacey Allen of "Color and You" (timallen@cheshire.net) in Walpole, New Hampshire, has been a color analyst for a number of years. Her mother, who had already been trained to do colors, started her off. Between them, they've done approximately seven thousand people's colors (six hundred were men!). Stacey spends two hours with each client, determining his or her skin tone. Then she categorizes the client as spring, summer, fall or winter. After that, she does a makeover using the correct tones for their skin and shows them a sampling of their colors. The client walks out with a palette of sixty colors they can choose from when shopping for clothes.

The two hours Stacey spends with each client is as rewarding to her as it is to her patrons. "I am able to show them how to look their very best," says Stacey. "And when one looks their best, one feels their best. Harmony, whether in life or in color, is more pleasing than conflict. You never get a second chance to make your first impression, so why not look your best? Life is simpler when you're in harmony—from packing to go on a trip, to buying lipstick, to having a home that feels good to every bone in your body—it all has to do with color. And it doesn't cost anything more to buy the colors that make you look great than ones that are just okay."

What does this have to do with interior design? Well, if you're comfortable with the color of your surroundings, you will be happier and, therefore, healthier. Not only will you feel good, you'll look good, which in turn will make you feel good, and around and around we go.

If you don't believe me, try this experiment. Go to your closet and look at your wardrobe. At first you might think that it's a hodge-podge of mismatched clothes. Take a closer look. There may be a pattern there of favorite colors. There are also a few items in your closet that when worn get you a lot of compliments. Think about it. If you look good wearing these colors, you'll look and feel good surrounded by them as well.

"That's the way uh-huh uh-huh I like it."
—Kool & the Gang

Some color experts will of course add to this experiment. Remember, our color preferences are also based on certain attachments, such as a favorite color that reminds us of Grandma's house or other good childhood memories. So think back. What colors 'feel' good to you, and

101

then try to think of why they feel that way. Those colors will make you feel good again if you incorporate them in your home.

Surrounding yourself with the right colors will brighten your appearance, making you look younger, rested and happy. The wrong colors will make you look sallow. So it stands to reason that if you're sitting in a black leather sofa, backed by gray-white walls, and these are not your colors, you will look ashen and out of place. This contemporary setting might look great in a magazine, but if it doesn't complement you, you're not going to enjoy owning it.

Want to check your color preferences against a worldwide, cross-cultural survey? First write down these colors: yellow, orange, violet, blue, red, and green. Now rewrite them in order of your preference. Don't read on until you have your colors categorized.

Okay, here we go. A scientist by the name of T.R. Garth surveyed a number of individuals of varying cultural backgrounds, asking them what colors they liked. From best liked to the least liked, the Native Americans preferred red, blue, violet, green, orange, and yellow. The Filipinos line up was red, green, blue, violet, orange and yellow. African Americans preferred blue, red, green, violet, orange and yellow. Caucasians had the same order of preference as African Americans.

Chapter Nine

Color
Language

"Try? There is no try. There is only do or not do."
— Yoda

Color is a universal language. It talks about romance, expresses cheerfulness, puts a smile on your face or, literally, brings on the blues. Color is everywhere; we can't escape color. Decorators and designers, florists, gardeners, salespeople, architects and fashion executives all require a familiarity with the language of color. But sometimes it's hard for laypersons to articulate the colors they'd like to have in their home environments. Using words to characterize a visual experience is inevitably hard, unless perhaps you've been trained in art and design. Even some of the basic terms like creating balance or harmony in a room or choosing textures or a contrasting color choice can seem foreign to the non-expert.

Here's an exercise you can try that might help you when conversing about color.

Make a list of words that describe the mood you'd like colors to evoke in your surroundings. (Examples: inviting, powerful, happy, soothing, romantic.) Close your eyes and think about each word for a second. What color comes to mind as your consider each word? Write it down next to the corresponding word. Now make a list of the rooms in your house and associate one or more of those moods to each room. The colors that correspond to the mood will give you a starting point for decorating those rooms. Keep this list and bring it with you when you are choosing paint or buying pieces for a particular room.

Creating Ambiance

So what do we do when we want to color our homes? After all, we want to be comfortable and feel "at home" there. Should we go for childhood memories? Should we go for a look that depicts who or what we aspire to be? Sometimes it is

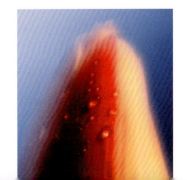

hard to decide what colors to choose when decorating our homes or choosing bathroom wallpaper or towels or even what color dishes to buy. The best choices are the colors you feel comfortable with, regardless of what's in or out of vogue, regardless of what your neighbor, cousin or best friend might prefer, regardless of what you think perhaps you should choose. But what if you like all colors and find it hard to pinpoint just what would be best for your home? It might help if we choose a mood, like we did in the exercise above, and then follow with the colors.

If a calm and peaceful atmosphere is desired, go for blue, lavender or green. These colors all work well together so if you're undecided, use all three. Variations of these colors work toward a peaceful atmosphere, too. Take teal, for example, which is a combination of blue and green and deep purple as in the colors of plum or eggplant.

If a warm motif cuddles up your mood best, go for rose, buttery yellow, peach and mocha. A romantic atmosphere can be had with these colors, particularly if the fabrics contain a combination of these colors in the form of flowers. If a less feminine look is desired, these colors can still be utilized in solid fabrics such as a golden hay colored sofa trimmed in rust. Throw a couple sunset coral colored pillows on it and the room starts to take on warmth.

Light and airy rooms work well in warm climates as well as in colder areas in a sunroom. The colors of choice here are a pastel version of yellow (not the warm buttery one) soft pink, light blue and coral, which is more of a pinky peach. These colors all do well as backgrounds such as on walls. A room painted light pastel coral will automatically make the room feel light and airy.

A down to earth look could be interpreted as cheerful and friendly. To accomplish that, go for bright blues, bright sunny yellows and terra cottas. Blue as in sky, yellow as in sun and terra cotta as in clay from the earth. See the picture?

For a more sophisticated look go for gold. Antique gold, hunter green, royal purple, royal or navy blue all fit into this luxurious, sophistication with grace and charm. In design, it is usually best to choose three colors; one as the theme, with the other two as accents. Combine any three of these colors and the look of lavishness will prevail.

As you can see, if you want to evoke a mood, say it with color.

Creating Balance

The best way to balance the color in a room is to maintain a three-color scheme. One color will be the main one while the other two are secondary. If you use the main color mostly throughout the room with the two secondary colors as supports to the first one, you'll have a balance in the room. Sometimes you've done that and you can still feel there's something wrong. Try moving one item—for example, a red vase—to another part of the room. It might just feel better on the opposite wall. This three-color scheme can be varied through the home. You can take one of the secondary colors and make it the primary color in another room using the other two colors that are left as secondary colors. In this way you can have a variety throughout the house while maintaining a good color flow.

Another way to achieve balance is to add live or artificial trees and plants. A room can be filled in and feel more welcoming with plants and trees. Green seems to fit in to any décor when it is in the form of foliage, as it tends to round off and complete a room.

Creating Contrast

Contrast can be bold or subtle. Yes, it can be subtle. Picture this: An office with light tan grass cloth on the walls, light tan Berber carpet and dark mahogany wood furniture. There it is, subtle contrast. The contrast is there yet it doesn't jump out at you.

Bolder contrast can be achieved by painting all the wood trim in white with the walls in any deep toned color. Or reverse that. Picture navy blue baseboards, doors and trim with soft yellow walls.

Contrast is easy to achieve. All you need to do is take a light shade and couple it with a dark shade. The contrast is bold if the colors are well removed from each other on the color wheel. The contrast is subtle if the same color family is used in light/dark combination.

A Word About Texture

If I were a musician, I might say that texture is a pattern of musical sound created by tones or lines played together. If I were an English major, I might say that texture is a composite of the elements of prose or poetry. Since I am an interior designer, let me say that texture is character. How so? Let's delve into this a bit.

Basically, there are two types of textures: smooth and rough. Smooth implies refinement, while rough depicts a casual atmosphere. Think of smooth satin, velvet, highly polished wood, glass, crystal, polished brass or chrome. What comes to mind? Puttin' on the Ritz, perhaps. When you think of it that way, it is easy to see how smooth textures equal formality, sophistication and refinement.

Now think of heavily stuccoed walls, rough-hewn beams, wide-planked and pegged wood floors, nubby fabrics. So start the fire and bring on the popcorn and beer. No ties required in this room. As a matter of fact, bare feet are welcome.

Generally, a room is either formal or informal, but take care not to go overboard in either direction. A formal look can come across cold if too much shine and slickness are used. If you find your room to be in this predicament, you can quickly and easily soften the tension by adding foliage. A tall tree or two with several smaller plants proportionally placed throughout will enhance the look of the room as well as make it more inviting.

On the other side of that coin, a room that is too informal might invite sloppiness on the part of the inhabitants. If the popcorn spills, there might not be an urgency to clean it up.

Contrast in textures affects more than just mood, though. A smooth, shiny texture appears lighter and less cumbersome than a rough surface. For example, a glass and brass cocktail table will tend to "float" whereas a dark mahogany one takes up more space visually.

To shrink an oversized room, use rough textures, as they tend to advance and dominate your visual spectrum. A ceiling that is too high can be "lowered" by adding beams. A nubby or thickly textured area rug will define a space, creating an atmosphere of 'come, sit by me'.

Time to flip that coin again. To make a small room expand, use light, smooth, airy textures. Glass, mirrors and smooth surfaces negate bulk and add illusionary space.

So how does texture fit in to a color book? A heavy texture will make the colors in it seem less intense as the broken surface will disperse the light and diffuse the colors. A satin pillow on the other hand, will reflect light showing the colors brightly. Picture this. A chenille fabric that is tan with an underlying thread of brown will appear as a tan fabric. The darker supporting color under it just enhances the tan somehow but doesn't really make much of a visual appearance. Take that same tan and brown combination and visualize it on a cotton chintz and you will clearly see two distinct colors in one fabric.

Design Tip
An overpowering sofa can be brought to manageable size by upholstering it to match the color of the wall behind it.

Color in Our Everyday Language

Even in conversation, color is used for emphasis. "Green with envy" is a descriptive phrase, yet trees are green and no envy is showing there. When someone is described as having a "yellow streak" it means cowardice, yet there is nothing wimpy about a golden yellow sunset. There seems to be no natural basis from which these sayings took their origin, yet we all understand what is meant when someone "sings the blues".

How many of these phrases are you familiar with?

A red-letter day is one of special importance.

To paint the town red means to celebrate.

Seeing red typifies being angry.

A red herring is a distraction that takes attention away from the real issue.

The "red eye" is an overnight flight.

Being in the red in business means losing money.

A greenback is slang for a U.S. dollar bill.

If you're given the green light, it means you can go ahead.

The green-eyed monster equates to jealousy.

A greenhorn is a newcomer or unsophisticated person.

Being green around the gills is to look pale and sickly.

Green with envy means full of envy or jealousy.

A person with a green thumb is good at gardening.

Someone true blue is loyal and faithful.

Talk a blue streak means to chatter incessantly.

Sing the blues means feeling sad.

Something out of the blue comes from an unknown source or at an unexpected time.

A bluenose is a strict, puritanical person.

A bluestocking is a scholarly woman.

To have a yellow streak means to have cowardice.

A white knight is a rescuer.

A white sale is a linen sale.

Tickled pink means feeling happy.

Someone black-hearted is an evil person.

If a business is in the black, it's making money.

To be blacklisted is to be boycotted.

A black tie event is formal.

Blackmail is getting things by threat.

So now that we've talked about all the ways in which we use color in our speech, let's see how we can "talk in color" to better express ourselves. Can we actually develop a color vocabulary? If we look at the list above, I'd say we already have.

Think of how you want your home to look. Bright, airy, cheerful, rich, elegant, inviting are words that might come to mind. That's a great start. Now let's attach color to those adjectives.

Bright could be bold colors such as the primaries of red, yellow and blue. It can be green, orange, or purple, too. Be careful what you ask for. Bright could be soft, light colors such as pale pink, soft yellow, peach or teal. Yes, that could be bright. It could also be airy.

Airy could be pastels, mostly whites or off whites. It could also be open and a little on the sparse side with furniture, having little to do with the colors used.

Rich could be dark, bold colors. Rich could be black, tan and gold. Rich could be purple, teal and brass. Rich could be deep green and tan. These same colors could be descriptions of elegant, also.

Design Tip

Need to add a little cheer to a room? Lots of natural sunlight is ideal. Remove the window treatments or at least bring them down to a minimum and let the sun shine in. Bright, strong colors are in order. Don't be afraid to be bold. A strong color on the walls will be seen more effective if the wood trim is another strong color. And don't stop there, go ahead and decorate with bold, colorful fabrics and accessories. Even brightly colored wood furniture can be fun.

113

Inviting? Well, that depends on what is inviting to you. Better come up with colors to describe what you really want.

So you see, with just these few examples, we see that color describes the mood with better accuracy. It might seem like an impossible task for some but it really isn't that difficult. Think of the mood (bright, airy, etc.) then attach colors that "feel" right to you in that mood.

You can practice by viewing rooms you walk into with a new eye. Go to model homes. Feel the mood then become aware of the color combinations. Go to open houses of homes that are for sale. Do the same test with mood and color. Check out a nice hotel. What is attractive about it? Is the mood right for you? If so, what are the colors used. Is it the furniture or is it a combination of furniture and the upholstery used on that furniture?

The more you think in color, the better you will get at developing a color vocabulary. The bright, airy, cheerful, etc. descriptions are a way to start, but then we need to add the color vocabulary to complete the picture.

When coloring your interiors, I can give you a panacea. Here it goes! Ceilings should be white or slightly off-white. Walls should be beige or light shades of peach, pink, pale yellow, soft green or soft aqua. Accent colors can include coral, green, blue or violet—with varying degrees of intensity. Why these particular colors? Well, it has been proven that when several people are gathered in one room, exposure to these colors are most comforting.

114

Chapter Ten

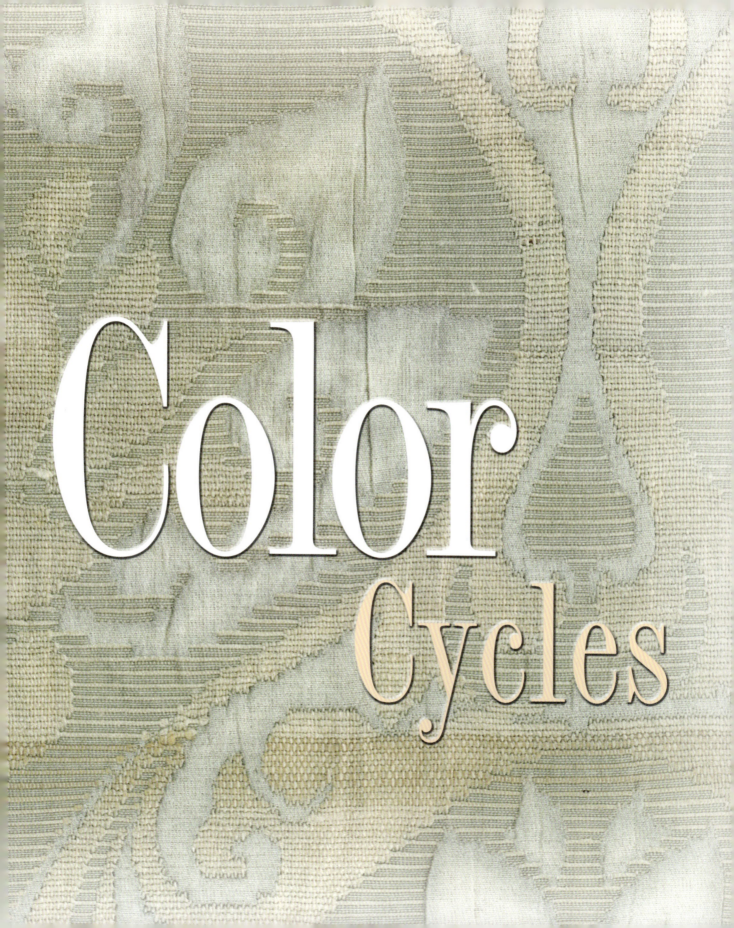

Color
Cycles

Color direction *can be described as the tendency a color family may be expected to take in the consumer marketplace in nineteen months or more.*

Color trends come and go as we know, but what makes this happen? Let's take a look.

Do you believe that everything that goes around comes around? This is true with colors. They go through definite cycles depending on fashion, technology, economy and other influences such as media and the arts.

Color trends sometimes run parallel with the decades. In clothing, color preferences might change within a decade but mostly they stay within the same grouping with slight variation to the hues.

There are color cycles in many things including fragrances. When greens are popular, lemon-lime scents are also popular. If the current craze is for red in fashion, then you might find Oriental fragrances finding their way into the scent scene. If feminine floral patterns are hanging on all the department store racks, then floral fragrances will dominate the selling chart. It seems we like harmony in everything. Love makes the world go round and harmony makes it spin smoothly.

So now let's check the evolution of the color palette over several decades and see if what's old is new again.

In the 1920s Art Deco was introduced at the 1925 Expositions des Arts in Paris. It would have a big influence in color and design over the next decade. In fashion you had Chanel who used a lot of black, white and beige. The flappers showed off their independence with royal purples, bright cherry reds, emerald greens and peacock blues. Interiors took on a monochromatic flair with their pale greens, blues and yellows.

In the early 1930s with the depression, browns were popular. Then in the post-depression years, white appeared on the scene in a big way, both in fashion and interiors. It went out of vogue by the mid-'30s and color gradually returned to fashion and furnishings.

At the start of the war, there were a lot of strong colors in fashion, including red, yellow and navy. As soon as paint, fabric and dyes got scarce, colors became muted and more limited. The 1940s also brought about the heyday of Hollywood and all its fantasy so pastels were in vogue.

The 1950s had a love affair with Hawaii so the colorful Hawaiian colors were very well received. Hot Pink became the rage as soon as Revlon started their "Paint the Town Pink" cosmetics campaign. It turned up in home furnishings and sheets and towels. Even pink and turquoise appliances became available.

> *"It's like deja vu all over again."*
> —Yogi Berra

Flower power exploded in the 1960s, bringing on the ever-popular psychedelic, neon colors such as acid yellow and funky purple. Oh, yes, funky purple was not only used in clothing but also in interiors. It was a very popular bathroom color. Yellow found its way into the kitchen in the form of harvest gold appliances and that yellow gold was often coupled with orange on the walls.

Basic beige was the color of the '70s. Earthy colors in general depict that decade. Interiors combined chocolate and cream as did fashion. The color world was harmonizing with the earth in browns, terra cotta, wheat, sand, camel and cinnamon colors. Harvest gold and avocado green appliances yielded to almond. But by the end of this decade, strong colors reigned once again. Neon fabrics and lights invaded the discotheques. Red, royal blue and turquoise became the new fashion colors. Who among us doesn't remember turquoise jewelry? If you don't remember, just go to your local department store and see the retro jewelry of choice. It's turquoise.

This explosion of color brought us into the 1980s. The Nancy Reagan red was big. Design directions were many, in the form of revivals such as Art Deco and Oriental influences. Do you still have mauve, peach and/or seafoam in your house? Those were the colors of 1981 and 1982. The brightness of the '50s returned with retro furnishings and design. Remember Miami Vice? Teal was the deal.

In the '90s we found a return to nature. Concerns about the environment and progress in technology were major influences on the decade. Greens and warm beige saw a revival. Earth tones were back in style. Romantic colors like lavender, rose tones and blues also emerged.

As technology continues to advance into our homes and offices, what will we be seeking next you ask? Balance, harmony and comfort are all words that come to mind. Indeed, 2001 was characterized by a new wave of soft colors, led by blue, aqua and true lavender. This was apparently in response to our desire—we the consumers—for more tranquility in our environment. The names of the colors alone are enough to make you want to curl up and relax— Cocobola, Capri Blue, Blue Too, Silver Strand Blue. Smudged Green? Well, with the supposedly six million hues that the human eye can discern, there are an infinite number of color possibilities and obviously new names to give them.

Design Tip

Small, square rooms will do well if two opposite walls are painted the same color, preferably an intense one. The deep color will create a feeling of depth.

Color is a major stimulus that affects our decision-making about countless things. No wonder it's such a big marketing concern among corporations. Using the right colors can literally make or break a business. It can attract potential customers—or not! Think of it this way: Let's say you run a small boutique. Your window display is enticing. Your awning is a color that draws people into your shop. Once inside, you want to keep them there, right? So even the color of the walls needs to be psychologically effective.

As we move toward an increasingly global society we are seeing color trends change more rapidly than ever before. Where do color trends come from? Who are the forecasters? There are associations and marketing groups that determine much of what we see out there in the marketplace. Two of the most influential are The Color Marketing Group (CMG) and The Color Association of the United States (CAUS). These organizations forecast colors two years

in advance of a selling season, and then clothing, housewares, furniture and many more industries incorporate these colors into the making of their products.

The CMG is an international, non-profit association of more than 1,700 color and design specialists who identify and forecast color trends for all products and industries. It was founded in 1962 and is based in Alexandria, Virginia.

The Color Association is the oldest color forecasting service in the U.S. Since 1915, the Association has been issuing color reports. Margaret Walch, Director of CAUS (they cover environmental/interior colors, women's fashion, children's clothing and menswear), gives insight into how it works with her agency. They have four different panels to select the shades for their areas of forecast. Each panel is made up of eight to ten members of the particular industry served. The association selects the panels, who assist gratis. Members must work in the U.S. and be leading colorists in their field of design.

"Color directions are never dictated, but suggested. If a suggested palette is not accurate—not a valid and reliable prediction—it will be ignored," says Walch. "Color cycles in fashion are roughly three to five years; in interiors ten to fifteen years, depending on the economy and other factors. Fashion forecasts are issued in September and March for spring and summer and fall and winter respectively; the association's interior forecast is issued in late September. This coordinates with how long it will take manufacturers to have the fabrics and/or other materials ready for a given season."

Why are Chinese food containers red? Because we associate China with the color red, so to make their food seem more authentic in our heads, it is packaged in red containers or white with red lettering.

Why does Dodge advertise all their vehicles as red? Because in our heads red cars are hot and they go fast. The same psychology applies to bicycles. Red ones feel like they ride faster and perhaps that is why it is the most popular selling color of bikes.

Why do many sugar companies package their product with blue on the label? Because somehow, blue triggers our sweet tooth. This is proven by sales records, even though our sweet taste buds are heightened when desserts are surrounded by the color pink, blue on the sugar labels outsold pink on those same labels 2-1.

Then there's the latest color craze associated with food products. Have you heard of it? Green and purple catsups by Heinz. Pink and blue squeeze margarine from Parkay. And sparkles for your yogurt by Dannon. You stir them in to get a boldly colored treat. Industry watchers are saying to expect to see more unexpected hues in otherwise commonplace food products.

Do you want to be a step ahead of everybody? Are you wondering what *the future* will bring? Then check out www.colormarketing.org or www.colorassociation.com

Happy hunting!

Here's an interesting tidbit about color trends and preferences. I spoke with Kelly Herkalo from M&M/Mars consumer affairs and asked her how the M&M company chooses the colors for their delicious little chocolate morsels. The whole selection is based on us, the consumer. They put out consumer preference tests and compile the results and with that they color their chocolates. But, get this, each product has its own color preference according to and dictated by the consumer. M&M Crispies have 16.6 percent blue ones while blues in M&M Plain take up 10 percent of the color combination. M&M Peanut are made up of 20 percent red ones but M&M Mini's only have 12.5 percent shelled in red. Overall, though, brown is the most chosen color, perhaps because it reminds us of chocolate. I had to ask about blue because it seems to stand out from all the other colors. Here again, they put it to the public. M&M/Mars had a "Vote For Fun" campaign and the color choices were blue, pink, purple or no change. Blue won. Have you noticed that tan is no longer in the mix? Blue replaced it.

Chapter Eleven

Color
Questions

FAQs

Q. How can I make a small room appear larger?

A. The use of color can open up a small room. Use light, cool colors for the walls and upholstery. The light colors seem to open the space and will also make the furniture seem lighter (as opposed to a heavy look). Also, use colors and fabrics that blend rather than contrast.

Q. My house is one big open space. There are few defining walls. How do I create intimacy and coziness?

A. Take advantage of bold colors, patterns and textures here, as a large, open room will carry these aggressive items well. Accent one wall with a bold color or patterned wallpaper for drama and attention.

Q. I have support columns right in the middle of my living/dining room. How can I make them disappear?

A. Don't. Instead make them a focal point by faux painting them. The faux paint can be as extravagant as a jungle scene complete with trees, monkeys and a few other critters. Or it can be as simple as sponge painting using two or three colors from the room's color scheme.

Q. My big screen television is really, really big and seems to overpower the room. What can I do to make it look not so out of place?

A. *Darken the wall behind the TV. This can be done with paint or darkly colored wallpaper. The television will then seem to sink into the background.*

Q. New houses have nice, tall ceilings that make them feel open, but my old house has lower ceilings. How can I make the rooms seem more open without remodeling?

A. *Raise the ceiling with vertical shapes on the wall. Paint stripes on the wall or wallpaper with a pattern that makes your eyes go up or use tall, vertical pictures on the wall. Any of these tricks will create the height illusion you're looking for.*

Q. My family room has no character. What can I do?

A. *Dull spaces can be brought to life with a bold pattern. One bold pattern should be enough, particularly if you are not real experienced at mixing and matching patterns. Small, complimentary prints will support your bold one and one or two solid-colored fabrics will complete the look. Another way to fire up the room is with bold colors. Choose one wall and paint it bold, use neutral upholstery and splash them with pillows of a multi-colored print. Be sure the bold color on the walls is also one of the colors in your colorful pillows. The floor should be the same neutral color as the upholstery, with perhaps splashes of color on the border of the rug, carpet or painted floor.*

Q. My house is chock-full of odd angles, sloping ceilings, alcoves, nooks and crannies. How can I make it less messy?

A. Two things can be done. If the busy architecture bothers you, go nude. No, not you. The furnishings. Beige on beige, or white on white, or gray on gray—need I go on? In other words, a monochromatic look will smooth, camouflage and add sophistication to the place. Keep the furnishings simple and do not over crowd the rooms. If, on the other hand, you love all the architectural adornment, then accent with color. For example, if you choose to paint the majority of the walls a pale peach, accent the alcove in a deeper shade of peach. Accentuate the varying levels by using different textures. Create wood frames around the various angles and paint them an accent color. You can further add to the frame idea by creating "picture frames" on walls where there will be no pictures. Just attach simple molding in a square or rectangular shape to a solid wall, and paint it the same accent color as your angled frames, window or doorframes. Furniture should still be kept simple, but in this scene, prints on upholstery and leggy tables and chairs will add to the variety.

Q. My bedroom ceiling is too high and I feel lost in the room. How can I fix this?

A. Lower the ceiling by painting it a slightly darker shade than the walls. A subtler approach is to shade the walls so that they darken as they rise to meet the darker ceiling. This is tricky to do but is very effective. Add a chair rail to divide the wall.

Q. How can I make my house look like a professional designer did it without having to pay for design service?

A. Since you've purchased this book, you've already paid me so you deserve a good answer to this question. Take an upholstered piece in the room that has the perfect fabric on it. Take the lightest, palest shade from that fabric and duplicate the color on the wall. Use a brighter hue from the pattern for another upholstered piece such as an occasional chair. That same

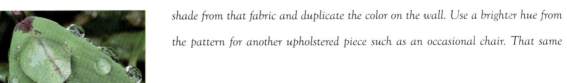

color can be used on the window treatments and also on the moldings in the room. The brightest, boldest color should be reserved for accessories such as knick-knacks, throw pillows, window treatment accents and matting on pictures. Like it so far? Before going ahead with this scheme, think of how this would work in reverse where the boldest color is used on the wall and the palest for accessories. Aggressive? Yes. Both ideas work equally as successfully; all you need to do is decide which way the room will be most appealing to you.

> *"...originality consists of new combinations, and not of the creation of something out of nothing."*
> —Richard V. Clemence

Q. My husband loves dark colors, particularly blue and I love soft, wispy colors. How can we compromise?

A. Deep blues mixed with tans work great in a home. The combination gives a strong, masculine feel and can be dressed up or down depending on what the lifestyle in that particular room will be. Dress down for the family room and dress up for the more formal living room. Reserve the wispy colors for the bedrooms. Most men will like even a master bedroom in soft, fluffy pastels.

Q. How can I give my house a new lease on life without breaking the bank?

A. Easy. Sometimes just a fresh coat of paint or new, colorful wallpaper will be all that is needed. Paint one or all walls a favorite color. Add a wallpaper border or some architectural molding and the room will look fresh and new.

Q. I have a room that is very narrow. What can I do to make it less closed in?

A. The trick is to fool the eye by painting the short walls dark and the long walls light. The darkened walls will seem to come into the room a bit, making them appear closer and therefore the room look a bit more in proper proportion. Next, place a bold print on one or both of those short walls to grab them and pull them in just a bit more. Furniture placement will help also. Don't put a long sofa on the long wall no matter how well it fits. That will only elongate the appearance of that wall. Instead, float furniture away from the short walls and make that furniture a solid piece, such as a love seat or an oversized chair, depending on what fits. Along the long wall, place two smaller chairs. This will "break up" the length of that wall making it appear shorter.

Q. I don't want to hire an interior designer because I'm only remodeling a bit, but want that professional look. How can I achieve this?

A. It's easier than you think. Say there's an upholstered piece in the room that has the perfect fabric on it. Take the lightest, palest shade from that fabric and duplicate the color on the wall. Use a brighter hue from the pattern for another upholstery piece such as an occasional chair. That same color can be used on the window treatments and also on the moldings in the room. The brightest, boldest color should be reserved for accessories such as knick-knacks, throw pillows, window treatments accents and matting on pictures. Like it so far? Before going ahead with this scheme, think of how this would work in reverse where the boldest color is used on the wall and the palest for accessories. Aggressive. Both ideas work equally as successful. All you need do is decide which way the room will be most appealing to you.

Q. I haven't the foggiest idea on how to begin planning the interior of my new home. What do you suggest?

A. *Don't fret. Just relax, sit back and browse through a few magazines. While browsing, rip out any pictures of rooms that are appealing to you. There need not be any rhyme or reason to this process, just go ahead and pull out everything that is attractive to your eye. After a while, you will start to see some type of pattern. Perhaps it is the colors in the room that entice you. Are they always bold colors? Are they always contrasting colors? Are the walls painted a light hue while the woodwork stands out in a dark hue? What about the furniture? Is it traditional, contemporary or a combination? In a short period of time you will have lots of magazine pictures and at least a general idea of what direction you would like to go in.*

"Imagination is the eye of the soul."

—Joubert

To get an exact color match, take the instigating fabric to a paint store that has a color computer and like magic, the hues and values of the mixed paints should come out perfect.

Chapter Twelve

Color
Success

"Do everything with so much love in your heart that you would never want to do it any other way."

—Yogi Desai

Forget trends. Don't go by what someone else tells you you want. Follow your heart. Here are a few incidents where the client's personal desires were used to the delight of the client and their friends/relatives even though the initial idea seemed really odd.

A bachelor wanted his place to be fun even if it was a little unconventional. He said he'd always wanted a swing in his place. A swing? Interesting. So we chose the living room for the manifestation of his dream. We suspended two porch swings from the ceiling facing each other, just like you might set two sofas or love seats to face each other in a "normal" living room. Then at the other end of the same room, we installed a billiard table. Well, not only did the client love the arrangement, but also all his friends thought it was the greatest room in town. The family room sported a regular leather couch and large screen television. Now that was the place to go for a party.

Then there was the lady that wanted plants in her winter home but since she only lived there a few months out of the year, she opted for artificial ones. She insisted they look as real as possible so the best of the best of silk plants were installed. When this lady left for her more permanent residence in the summer, she hired a house maintenance person to sort of keep everything working and clean. The plants were so real looking that the maintenance person watered them every week! Not until the water started leaking out did the maintenance person realize they weren't real.

Another lady absolutely loved the color purple and wanted everything in her house to be various shades of purple. She got her wish. The carpet was purple, the walls were pale lavender, the window coverings were of sheer material, violet of course, and the furnishings were mostly white so as to better feature the purple. The result? A magical princess looking home. She loved it and so did her friends.

In real estate, blue carpet seems to be a deal killer. Why? Who knows? I once was asked to decorate a model home and in my presentation I proposed blue carpet. One of the judging panel members brought up the fact of poor selling possibilities because of the blue carpet but the rest of the staff loved the complete package and were willing to gamble. We completed the home and it sold the first day it was open. The new owners then retained me to build a second story, add special cabinetry for their doll collection and even called me back year after year for little extras they wanted. Guess the blue carpet sat quite well with them.

Another couple wanted their dining room to be in the family room and the family room to be in the dining room. Confusing? Not really because it made sense to them insofar as they loved big tables for breakfast and sitting around during the day to read and work while watching television. The family room was bigger than the dining room so the big table went in there. Besides, they never did formal dining entertaining so a formal dining room would have been a waste. In the dining room we made a sitting area with four swivel chairs set in a circle and a cocktail table in the center. It worked for them and also attracted the Home and Garden show to video and broadcast the end product. The color theme presented in the foyer flowed through the new sitting room, which was right by the foyer. In the family room we continued the same colors in durable fabrics. Eggplant coupled with teal set the mood in this home.

Speaking of rearranging the room names in a house, another client had me eliminate the family room that was off the kitchen and make it the dining room instead. She loved to

137

entertain and her idea made perfect sense since the dining area was near where all the cooking and serving was being done. Then the originally designated dining room was turned into a library, complete with a library wall, library ladder, a small desk and a couple of very comfortable reading chairs. Where did we put the family room? We didn't. The living room was used as the family room with one wall dedicated to the television and other visual/audio components. For the color scheme, burgundy reds and sage greens were used to create a feeling of stability and grace yet allow entertaining without fear.

A guest bedroom is great to have but it does not necessarily have to read as a bedroom complete with bed, nightstand and dresser. A client bought a small home and needed every inch of square footage to be put to good use. Since she had overnight guests only once or twice a year, it seemed a shame to use the guest bedroom as only a sleeping room. Instead we used it as an office. It could also be used as a second family room for the kids, or a reading retreat. The sofa can be a pullout bed for when guests do stay. In our instance we used a futon instead of a pullout couch. We kept the colors calm and neutral so the room didn't scream with color when the occasional overnight guest would sleep there.

Powder rooms can be dark. Paint or wallpaper can be applied as dark as you want. If mirrors are an attractive option, black mirror is a great idea in the powder room. This room isn't used for shaving and it is not used for applying make-up or plucking eyebrows so dark

works just fine. In one home I used black mirrors on three walls with the fourth wall faux painted in black and gold stipple. The sink and faucet were gold plated and the toilet was black. It was an elegant restroom for guests. A fancy, elegant powder room will make guests feel special and, if that room is dark, it will feel glamorous, too.

138

Well-used family rooms do well with durable fabrics, of course, but should also have durable colors. What does that mean? Not pastels. One family had two toddlers that were fun-loving to say the least. They wanted the family room to be as childproof as possible. We opted for a darker shade of the color scheme we established throughout the rest of the house. The décor was bedecked with soft blues and yellows in the formal living room. We used navy blue coupled with a dark golden yellow in the family room. The toddlers' room was colored in primary blue and yellow, with a few accents in red.

Bedrooms always come across more inviting if they are decorated on the feminine side. Most men do not have a problem with a feminine master bedroom. One couple in particular actually requested that the master bedroom be as feminine and frilly as possible. The dust ruffle was made of layers of sheer fabric. The coverlet was floral pattern with matching floral draperies. The headboard was of an ornate brass pattern. The furniture was sturdy and big to give a strong, manlier support but we kept it on the feminine side by having it painted a white wash. The walls were painted soft peach to pick up one of the colors in the bedspread.

> *"Imagination is more important than knowledge, for knowledge is limited while imagination embraces the entire world."*
> —Albert Einstein

Many of my clients work at home. In these instances I always make one room a real office, not a guest room that serves as an office. This office does not have to match in color to the rest of the house. It can be dark wood or light wood with walls in grass cloth or floral patterns. The choice is yours but don't feel like you have to decorate it in an unbusiness-like manner just because it's part of the house. In one case, my client's business required a room where she could receive prospective customers. The room we used wasn't very big so we opted for a corner, L-shaped desk. With the desk at one end and out of the way, we were able to put a small table and two chairs on another wall so when my client was interviewing customers, she could sit with the person in a comfortable, inviting manner to discuss business, perhaps over a cup of coffee.

One thing I've found many clients love is a corkboard in, well, several places. In one teenager's room we put a wall of cork for pinning up pictures and souvenirs. This was a small wall between two doors but since we corked the wall from ceiling to floor, we had plenty of pinning space. Cork comes in rolls much like a wallpaper roll and can be applied right to the wall. In this same home we put cork in the office. We didn't have the luxury of a full wall like in the teenager's room but that didn't pose a problem. I bought a large frame, threw away the picture and inserted cork. I hung the newly revised 'picture' on the wall and there it was— instant corkboard. The reason for buying a frame is that this way you can make the corkboard as large or small as the space allows.

Resources & Recommended Reading

Albers, *Josef. Interaction of Color.* Rev. ed. New Haven, Connecticut: Yale University Press, 1975.

Birren, Faber. *Color & Human Response.* New York: Van Nostrand Reinhold Co., 1978.

Copestick, Joanna, and Meryl Lloyd. *Color (The Essential Style Guides)* Vol. 2. Alexandria, Virginia: Time-Life Books, 1998.

Cumming, Catherine. *Color Healing Home.* London: Mitchell Beazley, 2000.

Eiseman, Leatrice. *Colors for Your Every Mood.* Sterling, Virginia: Capital Books, Inc., 1998.

Grosslight, Jane. *Light, Light, Light.* 2d ed. Tallahassee, Florida: Durwood Publishers, 1990.

Hallam, Linda, ed. *Express Yourself with Color.* Des Moines, Iowa: Better Homes & Gardens Books, 1998.

Hope and Walsh. *The Color Compendium.* New York: Van Nostrand Reinhold Co., 1990.

Itten, Johannes. *The Elements of Color.* Translated by Faber Birren. New York: John Wiley & Sons, 1970.

Krims, Bonnie Rosser. *The Perfect Palette: Fifty Inspired Color Plans for Painting Every Room in Your Home.* New York: Little Brown & Company, 1999.

Luscher, Max. *The Luscher Color Test.* Translated by Ian Scott. New York: Pocket Books,

Mahnke, Frank H. *Color, Environment, & Human Response.* New York: Van Nostrand Reinhold Co., 1978.

McCauley, Mark. *Color Therapy at Home: Real-Life Solutions for Adding Color to Your Life.* : Rockport Publishers, 2000.

Mitchell, Shawne. *Feng Suhi: Ancient Secrets and Modern Insight for Love, Joy and Abundance.* Franklin Lakes, New Jersey; New Page Books, 2002.

Myss, Carolyn. *Anatomy of the Spirit.* New York: Crown Publishers, 1996.

Rossbach, Sarah. *Feng Shui: The Chinese Art of Placement.* New York: The Penguin Group, 1983.

Westgate, Alice. *The Complete Color Directory.* New York: Watson-Guptill Publications, 1999.

Quick Order Form

Fax orders: 239-261-7287

Telephone orders: Call 866-231-5900 (toll free)

E-mail orders: LMPublications@aol.com

Postal Orders: L&M Publications, PMB 229, PO Box 413005, Naples, FL 34103-3005

I would like to order _____ copies of Mystery of Color @ $34.95 each. (For quantity discounts and special sales please call our toll-free number.)

Name:_____

Address:_____

City:_____ **State:**_____ **Zip:**_____

Telephone:_____

E-mail address:_____

Sales tax: Please add 6% for books shipped to Florida addresses.

Shipping by air:

US: *$4.00 for the first book and $2.00 for each additional book.*

International: *$9.00 for the first book and $5.00 for each additional book (estimate).*

Payment: Check_____ Visa_____ MasterCard _____

Discover_____ American Express_____

Card number: _____

Name on card: _____

Expiration date: _____

Thank You for Your Order!